MY NAME USED TO BE MUHAMMAÐ

THE TRUE STORY OF A MUSLIM
WHO BECAME A CHRISTIAN

TITO MOMEN
WITH JEFF BENEDICT

ENSIGN
PEAK

Visit us at EnsignPeakPublishing.com

Library of Congress Cataloging-in-Publication Data

(CIP on file)
ISBN 978-1-60907-710-5

Printed in the United States of America
Publishers Printing, Salt Lake City, UT

10   9   8   7   6   5   4   3   2   1

MY NAME
USED TO BE
MUHAMMAD

CONTENTS

CONTENTS

AUTHOR'S NOTE

I was raised in a village in Nigeria where my family practiced a harsh form of Islam. When I was a teenager my father sent me to a radical Islamic school in Syria. Later I studied with members of the Muslim Brotherhood in Egypt while pursuing a degree in Islamic studies. It was there, of all places, that I discovered Christianity, a faith I had been taught to despise, along with Judaism. I am the last person you might expect to become a Christian. But I did. And for that I was disowned by my family and sentenced to life in prison.

That's right. My decision to believe in Jesus Christ cost me my family and my freedom.

But that decision also saved my life and taught me to believe in divine miracles. Some of my fellow inmates committed suicide. Some died of illness brought on by abuse and inhumane conditions. Others simply succumbed to hopelessness. But during my time behind bars, I never gave up hope. I never stopped believing. And after fifteen years I was released. That alone is a miracle.

I've written my story to shed light on the suffering of countless others who are victims of religious persecution. Freedom of expression and freedom of worship are sacred rights. Yet still in many parts of the world religious minorities are arrested, abused, or worse.

Although I was falsely imprisoned, beaten, and ridiculed, I don't harbor any bitterness. Nor do I blame Islam. I recognize that my life experience with Islam has been one of extremes in terms of intolerance and violence. But there are millions of good and sincere Muslims in many countries who love God and family while practicing Islam in a tolerant and positive manner. I consider them my brothers and sisters. At the same time, I am indebted to Jesus Christ and countless Christians from many sects and churches who have accepted me. This book is a tribute to their kindness.

ARRIVAL

I can feel the plane descending. My ears are filling up. My stomach is queasy. Below, a carpet of lights illuminates a sea of skyscrapers. I'd been told New York City was big, but I had never imagined it was this big. The buildings seem to touch the sky.

The passengers around me are asleep. It's 4:30 in the morning, and we've been flying all night. But I'm wide awake. Other than dozing here and there, I haven't slept. I haven't eaten much, either. Too much adrenaline. My nerves are a mess too. I pull my seat back forward and give my seat belt an extra tug. Nice and tight. I'm not scared. I'm elated. I'm over America.

It's been a long journey. Twenty-four hours ago I was in West Africa, eight time zones away. My name used to be Muhammad Awal Momen. Now my passport says Tito Momen.

CHAPTER 1

THE CHOSEN ONE

NOVEMBER 21, 1965
NGURU, NIGERIA

Wake up! Wake up!"

Startled, I sprang up in bed. It was 4:45 in the morning. In the darkness I could see my father's silhouette in the doorway. He had on his red Moroccan cap and an ash-colored gown over his trousers.

"We'll be late," he said. "Hurry."

Anxious, I slid off my handmade cotton mattress onto a colorful mat made of palm leaves and hit the light switch. A single bulb at the end of an electrical cable dangling from the ceiling illuminated the concrete floor and the scarce furniture in my room: a crude wooden wardrobe and a rickety wooden chair under a matching table with a kerosene lamp and a Qur'an on it. The room's only window was a two-foot-by-two-foot opening with three iron bars instead of a windowpane. It was my fifth birthday, and my presents hung from nails in the wall: white trousers, a long white gown, a white Moroccan cap, and a turban to wear over my cap.

I quickly dressed in my new outfit and grabbed my new string of ninety-nine plastic prayer beads, wrapping them around the fingers on my right hand. With my left hand I picked up my brand-new black leather sandals and headed for the door. My home was part of a compound that included six houses and a mosque. Relatives, mainly my uncles and cousins, owned the homes. My bedroom door opened to an outdoor walkway that led directly to the mosque. At the doorway I dropped my sandals over the threshold and onto the walkway. Then I stepped through the doorway, right foot first, and slid my feet into the sandals. Always exit and enter a room right foot first. Never wear shoes in the house. Those were the rules of Islam.

Careful not to step back into my bedroom with my shoes, I reached just inside the door and retrieved a blue kettle of water. Then I ran down the walkway to catch up with my father. Lean, wiry, and just under six feet tall, he had rich dark skin and walked with a slight limp.

"Good morning," he said impatiently.

"Good morning, Father."

"Do you have your Misbaha?"

I raised my right hand, showing him the prayer beads.

"Good," he said. "Dawn prayer is like starting the day with the Almighty."

I touched the tips of my beads and repeated the words: "Allah is great. Allah is great. Allah is great."

Arriving at the mosque, my father went directly inside. He had gotten up early enough to perform his ablutions at home. I ducked into the open-air washroom at the entrance to the mosque. It had a concrete floor with a round hole in it for urinating, as well as a water trough that led to an outside gutter. I squatted over the hole. Standing causes urine to splatter, which is forbidden because urine is considered unclean. A prayer offered by a man with urine splattered on his garment would not be accepted.

I left the washroom with my water kettle and rushed through the purification procedure known as Wudhu. I washed my right hand three times, then my left, before rinsing out my mouth and nose three times. Then I washed my face, ears, and feet. Clean, I looked heavenward and pointed with my finger. "I bear witness that there is no god except Allah alone, with no partner or associate, and I bear witness that Muhammad is His slave and Messenger."

Barefoot, I entered the mosque, clutching my beads. Individual rolled-up prayer mats lined the rear of the room. I passed through large wooden columns. Roughly thirty men from my village—all wearing trousers and V-neck shirts covered by full-length gowns, covered in turn by three-quarter-length gowns—were lined up in perfectly straight rows, kneeling on mats, facing the front of the mosque. My father was in the front row, on all fours, his eyes closed, his forehead pressed to the floor. I knelt on the mat beside him. A few feet in front of us, my uncle Othman (Oath-mun) knelt alone on a slightly elevated platform, his back to us.

Othman was our imam. We called him Sheik Othman. He was tall, slim, and bald with a long gray beard; his top front teeth were big and crowded. At 5 a.m. sharp, he rose to his feet, wearing a white gown and white trousers.

The moment he stood, everyone else stood and shouted: "Allah is great."

The imam raised his hands high above his head. "Allah is great," he said.

All of us put our hands above our heads.

"Allah is great," the imam said. "I testify that Allah is the only God, and I testify that Muhammad is his prophet."

"Allah is great!" we all repeated.

We all knelt back down.

"In the name of God, the Lord of Mercy and the Giver of Mercy," the imam began.

I repeated those words in my heart as the imam took us through the first surat in the Qur'an. Muslims perform five obligatory prayers throughout the day. The dawn prayer—or El-Subh—is the first one. And this was my first opportunity to do it. From that day forward I would be expected to rise before dawn and perform this prayer. No exceptions.

Forty minutes after arriving at the mosque, I returned home with my father to begin the day. We lived in Nguru, a town on the northern edge of Nigeria in Yobe State, nestled between the Sahara Deseret and a river flowing from Lake Chad. With around 150,000 residents, Nguru was connected to Lagos by rail and served as a hub for collecting and shipping ground nuts, cotton, meat, hides, and skins headed to Nigeria's capital city. The region's first modern slaughterhouse and refrigeration facility was erected there in the mid-1960s to process cattle and goats from outlying areas.

Our home was outside the city in a neighborhood called Hausari. It was predominantly Muslim, although there were some Christians, too. In fact, Christians built our home. It had cement walls with a zinc roof, wooden doors, and a cement floor. All the window openings were small and rectangular with iron bars. This design kept intruders out and allowed the desert air to circulate through the house.

The other homes inside the compound were identical to ours. Only the imam's residence was bigger and more elaborate, an indication of his status. His residence was an extension of the mosque. From my bedroom window I could see the mosque and a couple of forty-foot-high neem trees whose dark green leaves provided canopies of shade over the white desert sand that covered the ground all around our compound.

A few weeks after I started attending the mosque with my father, he came home from a business trip with a box full of writing exercise workbooks. Each workbook had about 150 blank lined pages. They were for practicing penmanship. "Keep these," my father told me.

Puzzled, I put them in my room.

The next day my father confronted me. "Where are the exercise books?"

"In my room."

"Good," he said, handing me a Qur'an. "Copy this book."

The thick book had a hard blue cover with gold lettering. It felt like an anchor when he placed it in my little hands.

All Muslims recognize the Qur'an as the supreme authority in Islam. It's the word of God as revealed through the angel Gabriel to the prophet Muhammad. The text is the basis of Islamic law and Muslim theology. Throughout his ministry, Muhammad recited the Qur'an to his followers. In keeping with that tradition, Muslims are expected to eventually memorize the entire text. Training begins at age six, around the time that children become school age. Those able to recite the entire Qur'an are known as *hafiz*. It's a distinction that is required to gain admission to top Muslim secondary schools in some countries.

Suddenly I realized why my father had given me all those writing exercise manuals. He expected me to get a head start memorizing the Qur'an by copying it word for word.

"Start with the 'The Opening,'" he told me.

The first sura in the book is known as "The Opening." It's very short. He recited it to me:

"In the name of God, the Lord of Mercy, the Giver of Mercy! Praise belongs to God, Lord of the Worlds, the Lord of Mercy, the Giver of Mercy, Master of the Day of Judgment. It is You we worship; it is You we ask for help. Guide us to the straight path: the path of those You have blessed, those who incur no anger and who have not gone astray."

"Praise be to Allah," I said.

"Praise be to Allah," he said. "Now, you copy until you can recite it."

"Yes, Father."

At that moment I commenced a daily routine of endless repetition, writing exercises intended to force me to memorize the Qur'an. Whenever I had nothing to do, I copied. Before bed, I copied. When I couldn't sleep, I copied.

These copying exercises were part of my father's dream. He believed in dreams, good and bad. Good dreams came from Allah and were viewed as revelation. Bad dreams were inspired by Satan and were never to be discussed. My father's favorite dream was a recurring one that always ended the same way, with my becoming an imam. In Arabic, *imam* means "leader." He leads the prayers and is generally regarded as the spiritual chief in the community.

But that wasn't good enough for the son of Abdul Momen. He had named me Muhammad Momen after the prophet of Islam. Proud and fiercely loyal to Islam, my father expected me to emerge as a leader among clerics, capable of leading a jihad, or holy struggle, to convert nonbelievers to Islam throughout our entire Nigerian homeland.

His dream for me was ambitious, even presumptuous. No one dared tell him that, though. That would have been an insult. Where I come from, insults are fighting words, especially insults directed at a man's family. To my father in particular, a man's reputation was a matter of life and death.

Like his African features, much of my father's personality stemmed from his roots. The son of a nomadic cattle herder whose ancestors poured into West Africa in the late 1700s, Abdul Momen was a member of the Fula tribe and a descendant of a sultan who came to power after Islamic spiritual leader Dan Fodio founded an Islamic spiritual community in Nigeria in 1809. A revered religious leader, Fodio took his people into exile and called for jihad against his oppressors. It became known as the Fulani War, which catapulted Fodio to prominence and led to the spread of Islam throughout the sub-Saharan African region, replacing paganism as the predominant religion.

Born in the 1930s, Abdul boasted that his ancestors were credited with introducing Islam into West Africa. He also didn't shrink from their reputation as nomadic cowboys, fearless men who drove cattle and goats through harsh desert terrain while holding fast to the strictest tenets of Islam. Abdul married young. By tradition, girls married between the ages of thirteen and sixteen; boys married by age twenty.

My father and his first wife started a family in Gashua, a large town located in northwest Nigeria, near the borders of Niger to the north and Chad to the west. My father started his career as a trader specializing in delicatessen and gourmet foods not readily available in the arid desert climate of northwest Africa. He'd journey to cities closer to the African rain forests, returning with yams, chocolate, honey, nuts, and other rare goods. Most consumers in Gashua couldn't afford his products. But my father wasn't after most consumers. He catered exclusively to the elite—Muslim spiritual leaders and the governmental leaders of Northeastern State (now known as Yobe State).

As the source of rare goods in high demand, he enjoyed great popularity among the ruling class. The most popular item he supplied was cola nuts. In Nigeria and throughout much of West Africa, cola nuts are symbolic and extremely important. Tradition holds that he who brings cola nuts brings life. And he who partakes of cola nuts partakes of life.

As a result, cola nuts are used to celebrate marriages, in much the same way that many Westerners use champagne. Cola nuts are also taken to funerals and given to the family that has lost a loved one. As a seller, my father knew a great deal about the nuts, which come from kola evergreen trees. The cola has a bitter flavor and a chemical composition that includes caffeine. Since Muslims are forbidden to consume alcohol, cola nuts are a popular substitute. But they leave a brown stain on teeth. That's why my father also sold miswak sticks, a chewing twig that whitens teeth and contains natural fluoride deposits and antiaddiction properties to combat the influence of caffeine. These sticks come from salvadora trees, which are native to the Middle East. Islamic tradition holds that the prophet Muhammad routinely used a miswak to clean his teeth and to give him strength while fasting. Muslims believe that besides preventing tooth decay and eliminating bad breath, the chewing stick cures headaches, increases vision, sharpens memory, and facilitates digestion if used frequently.

This sort of information flowed easily from my father. He had developed a comprehensive knowledge of his products, mastering even their chemistry and organic composition. He took the business of trading in commodities very seriously. The only thing he took more seriously was Islam. It was no coincidence that much of his inventory had some sort of religious connection. Islamic tradition, for example, held that the prophet Muhammad viewed the chewing stick as a purifying agent and a way to seek God's acceptance. Muhammad's views on miswak were contained in what's known in Arabic as *hadith*, basically narratives of the prophet's statements not found in the Qur'an.

These narratives are an essential element of Islamic law, and my father strictly practiced them. That had a lot to do with why his profession was so closely aligned with his ultimate mission—spreading the word of Islam. To him, there was no higher purpose in life. That's why he became so obsessed with raising up a son fit for the clergy.

When I was six, one of the most well-known imams in West Africa visited our mosque. Thousands of Muslims from nearby towns and cities came to hear him and be blessed by him. He gave a sermon that lasted through the night. My father took me, and at one point the imam placed his hands on my head. They were only there for a few seconds. But I felt honored, as if a holy saint had touched me.

The following day, my father led me into my bedroom for a talk. He pulled up a chair, and I sat on my bed.

"You saw how many people came to see that imam?"

"Yes, Father."

He poked his finger in my chest. "I want you," he whispered, "to be bigger than that someday."

It felt like his finger was going through my chest to my heart.

"He studied hard to get where he is," my father said.

I nodded.

"You must study harder. And with Allah's blessings you will get there."

I nodded.

"Don't let the evil one distract you."

"Yes, Father."

"No playing."

I nodded.

"No joking."

I nodded again.

"Pray *very* hard and take life *very* seriously."

He reached into his pocket and removed some dates. They were soft and plump. They were from Saudi Arabia.

"Thank you."

He reached into his other pocket and retrieved two shillings. He handed me those, too.

"Thank you."

Then he handed me a book. "This is another book for you," he said. "I will be traveling today. When I return, make sure you have read it and copied it. All of it."

He walked out.

I put the book down and ate some of the dates. They were juicy and delicious, unlike the dry, shriveled-up dates we had in Nigeria.

Then I flipped through the book. There were more than 200

pages. I knew I'd better get started right away. It would take days to copy all those pages word for word. I couldn't disappoint my father.

Before I was born, my father had two sons and a daughter with his first wife. Both sons were raised to observe the strict teachings of Islam, but they weren't groomed to become imams. My father was convinced that neither of them was the elect.

The boys were relatively young when my father's first wife died. It wasn't unusual for women in northern Africa to die before middle age. Conditions were rough, and women were perpetually pregnant. Plural marriage was also common, so the loss of one wife didn't work a hardship on the husband. His children were simply raised by his other wives.

Plural marriage is the only aspect of Islam that my father did not keep. I'm not sure why, but he remained monogamous. As a result, when his first wife died, he faced the prospect of raising two sons and a daughter on his own. With his heavy travel schedule, that wasn't going to work. Besides, like all the other men in his village, he wasn't accustomed to child rearing. Men eat, sleep, conduct their business, and practice Islam, which consists largely of performing prayers. Without a wife, he'd go hungry and his kids would go naked. So immediately after becoming a widower, my father went looking for a new wife.

That's when he met Hauwa (How-whah) Isa, a native Nigerian. In Arabic, *Hauwa* means "Eve." You wouldn't know she was a native by looking at her. She had very pronounced Arab features, such as jet-black straight hair and light skin. She married my father early in 1956. I don't know the exact marriage date or how they met. What little I do know is that their marriage wasn't born of romance. For my father it was a marriage of necessity. For Hauwa it was one of duty.

She conceived quickly and had a daughter named Amina. Four years later, on November 21, 1960, I was born.

My path to the clergy started that day. The minute my father laid eyes on me, he declared me the chosen one. He named me Muhammad Awal. *Awal* means "the first."

When I was four, my father put me on his knee and explained the significance of my name. "Peace upon him," he began. "You are named after the prophet Muhammad. You have a name to live up to."

He made sure I understood my responsibilities. "Lots of people name their sons Muhammad," he said. "Some fathers name all of their boys Muhammad. Muhammad the first. Muhammad the second. And so on. But in this house, you are the only Muhammad. Muhammad Awal means Muhammad the first. There will be no second. Not in this family. You must live up to that name."

My older half-brothers resented me because my father favored me. Over time, that resentment festered into hatred. But my brothers couldn't question my father's choice. At least not openly. Muslim fundamentalists in northern Nigeria take the view that fathers can select a favored son, irrespective of the boy's place in the birth order. My father subscribed to that view.

This touched off a classic Cain and Abel situation. My brothers didn't understand why they had been rejected. And I didn't understand why they hated me. Luckily, my mother spotted my vulnerability early on, and she worked hard to protect me from my older rival siblings. That made them resent her as much as they resented me. They saw us as the enemy. We even looked different from them. I had light skin just like my mother's. My hair was like hers, too—straight and black. My half-brothers had Afros like our father. It was easy to see that I was Eve's boy.

All of this made our family rather complicated. But my father was aloof from most of what went on. He was quite preoccupied. The same year that I was born, my father was appointed to be the spiritual advisor to the emir of Bade, who presided over an Islamic kingdom headquartered at Gashua. The emir was a traditional king who ruled under Islamic law. My father's post entitled him and his family to move into a home that was part of the palace compound in Gashua. We suddenly had access to servants and guards. Our home was always quiet and spotless. The same prisoners who were assigned to clean the governor's palace also cleaned our living quarters.

My father's position gave us access to the finest medical care. When I came down with malaria as a toddler, the sultan's physician attended to me, injecting me twice daily with drugs not available to the general public. I recovered and went on to develop a strong, healthy body. These were the perks of palace life and of being the son of a prominent trader who doubled as an influential spiritual advisor to the political elite.

I have little memory of living in the palace compound in Gashua. We moved from there when I was four. That's when we settled in the family compound in Nguru. My father wanted to be settled in Nguru before I turned five. That's the age when boys start attending the mosque. In the Muslim culture, age five is an important milestone in the development of a child. Boys begin to learn the rituals and prayers of Islam, and girls start learning to cook and clean.

Preparing, cooking and serving food occupies a significant portion of a young woman's life. At our home, the kitchen wasn't actually in the house. Cooking indoors just wasn't compatible with the oppressive desert heat. Instead, my mother cooked in an open-air kitchen twenty feet from our house. It had a roof to shield her from the sun, along with one wooden table for food preparation. There was a fire pit with a hearth consisting of three large stones. Clay pots containing water typically rested on the stones. The floor was white desert sand. Pumpkins, clay pots, and firewood often dotted the outskirts of the kitchen space. Closer to the fire, my mother typically had a goat or ram carcass. The smell of burning animal hair would waft through our home.

Her specialty was okra stew and rice with pumpkin. But she had a routine. Every day at noontime she would go out to meet a group of women from the village that were referred to as the dairy ladies. They always had two or three large calabashes, or gourds, stacked on their heads. These hollowed-out vegetables were used to transport fresh cow milk, yogurt, and *gwe* (gwee), our version of butter.

I never liked the milk—it was unpasteurized and often had cow hair in it. But the yogurt and gwe were like candy. My mother would routinely mix yogurt with millet balls, cassava grain, or the crust of rice or millet and feed it to me like a dessert. The gwe was used in soups and sauces.

Girls are required to be in the kitchen; boys are forbidden to go there. It's a woman's domain. Men and women don't eat together, either. In fact, our family never ate together. Each day at sundown, one of the imam's disciples bellowed into a loudspeaker that could be heard throughout our compound: "God is great. I testify that Allah is the only God and Muhammad is his prophet. Come along to pray."

Men and boys drop whatever they are doing and head to the mosque for the dinner-hour prayer. Women remain at the fire, putting the final touches on dinner preparations while listening to the imam's prayer as a disciple repeats it over the loudspeaker. Our imam usually kept the dinner prayer short. He did not like to wait for his dinner.

After prayer, men spill out of the mosque, take their seats on the deck of the veranda, and wait for their daughters to serve them. The imam had four wives, each of whom served as chief cook on alternating days. Since my father had just one wife, my mother cooked every day, and she dutifully sent the best portions of meat to my father and the men who were eating with the imam.

Boys ate together in the courtyard between the houses and the mosque. My sisters always served us boys after the men. I had my own special plate. It was a metal bowl with a cover that had a flower on top. We didn't have utensils. We ate everything with our hands, including rice. We didn't have cups or mugs, either. We drank from hollowed-out gourds. We'd fetch water from a well with a big clay pot and then pour it into a gourd. All of us children shared one gourd. The women had their own gourd to drink from. The same with the men. The imam drank from his own gourd.

My mother was always the last person to eat.

After dinner, the women washed the dishes and the men returned to the mosque for evening prayer.

Dress was another thing women had to concern themselves with. All the Muslim women in our community wore layers of clothes, exposing only their feet, hands, and face. It was a sin to display more of themselves than that, and in certain situations their faces had to be covered too. My mother always wore a long-sleeved, multicolored blouse and a black, ankle-length skirt. On top she'd wear a wrap that matched the blouse. She wore a red or yellow or green headscarf.

My mother was short and had narrow feet and small fingers. Her nails were kept extremely short. Only prostitutes had long nails. But my mother always had a pair of huge circular rings dangling from her ears. Most women had multiple piercings in each ear, some as many as twenty. My mother had only one hole per ear.

Feet and hands are about the extent of what I saw of my mother's body. Once in a while her lower arms were visible, as when she was cooking over a hot fire.

Whenever my father went away on business, he would bring back something for my mother. Typically it was an article of clothing, such as a headscarf or a wrap. Sometimes he'd bring her a piece of jewelry. Of course, my mother rarely had opportunity to wear these items in public, because she wasn't allowed out of the compound except on special occasions, such as the birth of a child or the death of a loved one. Women were expected to stay indoors or at the outdoor kitchen. They almost never ventured into town.

My father, on the other hand, was a big traveler. He was one of the only men in our neighborhood with a car. It was a light green Opal. That's what he used to transport his goods to and from the various cities where he did business.

One of the first gifts that he brought back to me from a business trip was a soccer ball. It was green and made of rubber.

My father loved soccer. We called it football, and it was my only diversion from religion. The day after he gave me the soccer ball, he saw me kicking it against the wall of our compound. At one point the ball bounced off the wall, and he intercepted it. "With football you need to learn to dribble," he said, advancing toward me as he kicked the ball. "If you can't dribble, you can't be a good football player."

He kicked the ball to me. I tried dribbling like my father. But I lost the ball. He retrieved it and dribbled again. "You must practice," he said. "Practice. Practice."

My fondest memories of my father involve our kicking a soccer ball together on the sand. It seems like we did it all the time. We really didn't. But those memories with my father are so bright that they tend to eclipse the other ones. Soccer was the only thing we did together that didn't have religious overtones. I liked that.

CHAPTER 2

HEAD OF THE CLASS

Hausari had three elementary schools. Two were private Christian schools. The third was called the Hausari Primary School and was open to anyone. It was within walking distance from our home. The British established it for Nigerian children in grades one through seven. Most of the imams in northern Nigeria frowned on Muslims attending English schools. As a result, many young Muslim boys were sent to train with members of the clergy in hopes that they would become true disciples of Islam. These boys often ended up being able to recite the Qur'an, but they knew nothing else. Meantime, they were subjected to harsh physical and verbal abuse at the hands of orthodox imams. By the time these boys became teens, many of them were in the streets begging for food. Hausari had packs of such boys living in the streets.

Like other financially successful Muslims in the area, my father insisted that I obtain a quality education, even if that meant attending a school where Muslims and Christians shared classrooms. The curriculum at Hausari was traditional in a Western sense, focusing on letters, mathematics, science, and foreign languages. A heavy emphasis was placed on reading and writing. Religion classes were also taught. Once a day the Muslim students would learn from an Islamic teacher while a Christian instructor taught the Christian students. Total enrollment was 588 students, with each primary grade divided into two classes of forty-two students. Boys were required to wear knee-length white shorts, white leather shoes, white caps, and short-sleeved shirts with a Hausari Primary School emblem on the pocket. Girls wore blue dresses.

I was six when I entered primary grade one in 1967. By that time I was fluent in Arabic and had already read the Qur'an in its entirety multiple times. I had also handwritten the entire text of the Qur'an.

Another reason I knew the Qur'an so well was that I had never been allowed to read anything else. My mother had been forbidden to read me children's stories, fairy tales, or nursery rhymes. Even children's education books about nature, animals, or African history were kept from me. My father wanted me reading the Qur'an and nothing else.

My reading list expanded when I entered school. I was required to read books about the stars and planets, world history and arithmetic. At the same time, I had to learn English. My instruction book was a collection of simple African folk stories written in English. I took the book home so I could practice reading the stories to my mother. One afternoon while she was making pasta, I sat at her feet and read the story of a girl flying a kite. Five or six children of Muslim friends from the neighborhood were at our house. None of them attended Hausari, and they were enthralled with what I was reading.

Suddenly my father entered the house. The children instantly ran out.

He looked down at me. "What are you doing?"

"We are reading," my mother told him.

He took the book from my hand. "You don't need to read this to other children," he said.

Then he turned to my mother. "You know this thing cannot be done here!" he whispered.

"They are children," she said. "He's studying, and they want to hear."

My father pounded his fist on the table. "No! Their parents don't want them attending that school. Western education is prohibited."

My mother nodded.

"If you want to study, you study alone," my father said, handing me back the book. "Go to your room and do it."

Another reason many Muslims in our area refused to send their children to Hausari was the presence of female teachers. My first teacher was Mrs. Abdul, and she quickly picked up on my enthusiasm for learning. She spotted something else in me—an artistic talent. At the start of the school year, she assigned our class to draw a flower as part of an art lesson she was teaching. I hesitated. At home, art was forbidden. Islam teaches that it is wicked to illustrate Allah with pictures. But my father took an even more extreme approach, insisting that *all* art was evil. As a result, sketching, drawing, and painting were strictly prohibited. I had never drawn anything, not even a stick figure.

With Mrs. Abdul's encouragement, I completed the first art assignment. When she saw my sketch, she couldn't believe that I had never sketched before. Comparing my picture to a photograph, she made a point of calling on me to draw things on the blackboard anytime she wanted to illustrate something she was discussing. Before long, I had become Mrs. Abdul's personal in-class illustrator and her favorite student.

Up to that point I didn't know I had a talent for art. But Mrs.

Abdul's encouragement fueled my desire to get better. She also told me I was the best reader among her forty-two students. That was probably due to my father's insistence that I spend so much time in the Qur'an. As a result, Mrs. Abdul selected me as the class monitor. This was a big deal. Each class in the school had one designated student monitor. It was a title of honor. Only the best students were selected for this position, which entailed presiding over the class whenever the teacher left the room.

The first time Mrs. Abdul turned the class over to me, she said she'd return in an hour or so. In her absence, students were expected to maintain absolute silence and complete an in-class writing exercise. I took my place at the head of the class and collected the papers upon completion. One boy—a six-year-old named Mustafa—began acting up almost immediately after Mrs. Abdul left the room. Three different times I told him to stop making noise. If Mrs. Abdul had been present, the boy would not have received even one warning. Corporal punishment was routinely applied to maintain order. Students were struck across the knuckles with a ruler, spanked, and made to do such things as stand still for hours while holding books in their outstretched hands.

Class monitors were expected to mete out punishment in the teacher's absence. I felt anxious about that. Violence didn't come naturally to me. The thought of using a ruler on a peer left me feeling guilty. So I let it go.

Toward the end of class, I told the students to turn in their papers. I glanced at Mustafa's and discovered that he'd barely done anything. Seven of the ten questions were left blank.

"Mustafa," I called out. "Come and get your paper."

He looked up at me from his seat.

"You didn't do anything," I said. "Come here."

His arms by his sides, he walked toward me as the class looked on in silence.

"Open your hand," I told him.

He hesitated.

Shaking, I reached for the wooden ruler. It felt awkward, the idea of hitting a classmate. But I was too scared not to at that point. My father had drilled into me a deep respect for authority and a strict adherence to rules. Mustafa had disobeyed. I had no choice.

He extended his right arm, the palm of his hand down.

Weakly, I whacked him across his knuckles.

"Ouch!" he said, flashing a mischievous grin. Then he hopped up and down, as if it was all a big game. Some students started giggling.

"Show me your hand again," I said. I brought the ruler down with all my might. *Clap*. The sound echoed through the classroom.

"Leave your hand out," I ordered.

Clap.

Clap.

Clap.

Tears streamed down his face, and no one was giggling anymore. I felt terribly guilty. But I kept a stern face.

"Now go sit down," I said. "I will tell Mrs. Abdul when she returns."

I never liked that aspect of being a monitor. But after I used the ruler once, each time thereafter got a little easier.

My father liked the school's approach to strict discipline. But he chafed over the fact that I had Christians in my classes. Most Christians sent their kids to one of the area's two exclusively Christian academies—St. Paul's and St. Augustine's. So only about 20 percent of our students were Christian. But that was enough for many of the men in our neighborhood to give my father a hard time. They were complaining to the imam, too, suggesting that the mingling of Muslims and Christians was having a corruptive influence on me.

My father was as outspoken as anybody that Western education was corrupt. But given where we lived, he felt he had no choice but to leave me at Hausari. He wanted me trained in English, the sciences, and math. No other non-Christian schools near our home offered those subjects.

To counter the wicked influence of Christian students and teachers, my father simultaneously enrolled me in an Islamic primary school that focused exclusively on Islamic and Arabic studies. The school was called Nur Awald. I went there every evening from 4 p.m. to 6 p.m. to study logic, Arabic, and the Qur'an. Basically, I spent six hours a day in a secular school and two hours each night in a religious school.

My Qur'an instructor was from Libya. He had a reputation for teaching students how to recite suras in a poetic voice. The first sura I memorized under him was titled "Joseph." I particularly liked one of the opening passages:

"Joseph said to his father, 'Father, I dreamed of eleven stars and the sun and the moon: I saw them all bow down before me,' and he replied, 'My son, tell your brothers nothing of this dream, or they may plot to harm you—Satan is man's sworn enemy.' This is about how your Lord will choose you, teach you to interpret dreams, and perfect His blessing on you and the House of Jacob, just as He perfected it earlier on your forefathers Abraham and Isaac: your Lord is all knowing and wise."

I liked this one so much because it reminded me of my situation. Like Joseph, I had older brothers who should have inherited the birthright. But my father had chosen me over them. His choice became my burden.

Neem trees played an important role in our village. Traditionally, after women give birth, they bathe multiple times a day for sixty days afterward. The neem leaves are used to scoop and splash hot water on the woman's body. This is done because it is believed that it is healthy and it keeps a woman's body young.

One particular neem tree with its roots out of the ground was my favorite. It was just across the street from our home, which was on one of the busiest streets in Hausari. I liked to sit on the roots and watch people coming and going to the nearby open market where animals were traded and food and other goods were sold. From that spot I also had a direct view of the veranda just off the front of the mosque. People were always gathering to chant or pray. Once a day the imam would emerge and take his place on a wooden chaise longue. He'd recline, rest his thick arms on a couple of decorative pillows, and minister to his followers.

Whenever the imam was on the veranda, women were not allowed to pass by on the street unless their faces were veiled and their shoes removed. It was a serious insult to the imam and to Islam to do otherwise. One afternoon a woman was on her way home from the hospital that was located a couple of blocks from our mosque. She had a sick baby in her arms and a nylon bag containing medicine over her shoulder. With her other hand she held the hand of a toddler walking beside her. Approaching the mosque, she slipped her feet out of her slippers. When she bent over to pick them up, she inadvertently squeezed her sick infant, causing it to cry.

As she tried to comfort the baby, her bag fell off her shoulder, causing the medicine bottles to spill onto the street. At the same time, her toddler imitated her by removing his shoes. It was midday, and the heat rising from the white street made the bottoms of his tender feet burn. He started crying too.

Attempting to lift the toddler with one arm, the mother nearly dropped her baby. Hearing the crying children, one of the men near the back of the audience listening to the imam finally went to her aid. He picked up her medicine and helped place the bag back over her shoulder. But the woman still had to stop and bow down when

24

she passed by the imam. Every woman had to. Meanwhile, the imam never noticed her. He was too busy talking to his disciples.

Muslim women where I grew up were used to being in a subservient role, one that kept them quiet and unseen for the most part. One of the worst things a woman could do was expose her body to anyone but her husband. Even at home, my mother never dressed down. In extreme heat she might remove her outside layer of clothing while cooking in the kitchen. Even then she always wore one layer to cover everything but her hands and face. I remember one incident when my mother was breastfeeding. Women were required to cover themselves with a blanket whenever they nursed their babies. On this occasion, my mother was seated on a bench under the canopy at our outdoor cooking area. While nursing she was keeping an eye on a big pot of stew and some meats that were roasting over the fire. Suddenly, my mother spotted my two-year-old sister crawling right toward the fire. My older sister had been keeping an eye on her, but my mother had sent her inside the house to retrieve something.

"Stop!" my mother screamed as she put her infant on the ground and rushed to the fire, snatching up my sister just inches from the hot flames.

My mother's breasts were exposed when her nursing blanket fell to the ground in her rush to rescue my baby sister. I turned away quickly, knowing I wasn't supposed to see her that way.

My father was drawn to the scene by my mother's scream. He arrived just as she was leaning down to pick up the infant, still cradling the toddler in her other arm. She was still exposed, and both children were crying.

"You are walking around naked!" my father shouted. "Are you out of your senses?"

As she scrambled to cover herself, my father backhanded her across the face. She stumbled but didn't drop the children. He walked away, and she collapsed on the bench to resume nursing.

That was the only time I ever saw my mother exposed. And I cried when my father beat her.

If a man other than my father had seen my mother's exposed breasts, her punishment could have been as harsh as death by stoning. Although not always the case in other parts of the world, the interpretation of Islamic law in our community considered it a man's duty to use violence to punish women who failed to properly cover themselves. I always felt guilty for not defending my mother when my father would beat her. But the cultural pressure to leave the situation alone was so entrenched that it stifled my sense of right and wrong. That only made me feel worse.

Once a woman in our village came to our home to braid my mother's hair. They were in the house, of course, when my mother remembered that she had left a pot of soup on the open fire out on the veranda. She dashed out the door to save the soup. Since her hair was half-braided, she didn't take time to put on her headscarf.

At that moment, my father passed by. He noticed she wasn't wearing her headscarf. "You are walking with a naked head," he said, backhanding her across the face.

My mother fell to the ground, holding her chin and crying.

"Next time cover your head," he said, standing over her. Then he walked off.

Humiliated, my mother buried her face in her hands. The woman who was there to braid her hair witnessed the encounter. I did too. My mother knew that we knew. It made me angry to see my father hurt my mother. But it wasn't as if I could stop him. Nor was my father's behavior unusual. Virtually all the men in my village exercised a strong hand with their wives. We didn't call it domestic violence. It was just domestic life.

Although it was acceptable for a husband to dominate his wife, a child would be severely punished for disrespecting his mother. In my home, the expectations were even higher. For instance, most boys in my village referred to their mothers as "mum." Not me. Not in my father's home.

I remember calling my mother "Mommy" only once. I was quite little. As soon as I said it, my mother hit me on the top of the head. Hard. "Don't you know my name?" she said.

My head throbbed. She never apologized, and I never called her "mommy" again.

"The name Eve is an honorable name," my father told me. "She was Adam's wife. So it is an honor to be named that."

Our culture was tough on children, too. On an average day, I was lucky to have an hour for leisure. My time was consumed with secular school, religious studies, and prayer rituals. Even at night, I was expected to spend a couple of hours, from 8 p.m. until bedtime, learning Islamic teachings from older family members.

My mind increasingly drifted to art. That was my passion. At the end of my first year at Hausari, I was awarded first prize for having the best drawing in my grade that year. At the end of my second year, I won first prize again. At that point, the school's headmaster presented me with a key to the school's art supply store. It was the sort of reward that inspired me to work hard to improve my drawing skills.

The headmaster, a slim, chain-smoking man with a very dark complexion, even singled me out in a student assembly and encouraged all students to find their talent and pursue it. I was eight years old, and being recognized like that gave me confidence and a sense of self-worth. With access to the school's art store, I began stockpiling supplies. Before long I discovered that watercolors were my favorite medium for illustrating nature scenes. I painted flowers, rivers, clouds, and sunsets. At the same time, I continued to sketch with a pencil. The more proficient I became, the more my teachers relied on me to illustrate objects from the lessons on the chalkboard.

I even started drawing at home in my bedroom at night. Of

course, I knew how my father felt about art, but I figured what I was doing was all right since it was school related. Sort of, anyway.

On one particular evening, I was sitting on a floor mat in my room, using crayons and a pencil to sketch. My back was to the door when I heard someone enter. I figured it was one of my siblings.

"What is that?" my father asked.

I immediately jumped to my feet.

He examined my sketch pad. It contained a half-finished picture of a pumpkin.

"It's schoolwork," I said. That wasn't really true. But his tone frightened me. And his eyes were steely and squinting. I was desperate to justify my sinful behavior. "It's an assignment."

"If it's for school, you should leave it there," he said. "Don't bring it here. Not drawing. I should not see them here anymore."

Hurriedly, I packed up my crayons and pencils.

"If I catch you next time with those here," he said, "no one can save you from my hand."

"I am sorry, Father."

It was months before I dared take art supplies home again. The only reason I did was that my father was away on business. I took advantage of his absences to draw in the privacy of my bedroom. It was more fun than anything I had ever done.

One evening while he was out of town, I was lying face down on my bedroom floor, drawing a picture of a neem tree. I must have been concentrating so much that I didn't realize someone had entered the room. Suddenly I was kicked in the ribs with such force that I flew off the ground and crashed into my iron bed frame. My head hit against one of the legs.

"Ouch!" I screamed as I turned over, ready to strike.

But it was my father standing over me. He'd come home early and found me drawing. Suddenly, I was frightened.

"I told you, and you didn't hear," my father said, kicking aside my picture. "Now you can hear it with your body."

He lifted me to my feet and slapped my face with his open hand. Then he backhanded me.

I screamed, prompting my mother to come running. As soon as she saw my father in a rage, she turned and left. She would have been beaten if she had aided me.

I covered my face with my arms just before he resumed smacking me. It lasted until he was out of breath. "Hhh . . . hhh . . . hhh . . . when I catch you next time . . . hhh . . . hhh . . . nobody can save you."

That was the last time I ever drew at home.

My Qur'an instructor at the private Islamic school also recognized my artistic talents and invited me to enroll in his class on Arabic calligraphy. I told him to talk to my father. In this instance my father approved, since the calligraphy was Arabic and the Qur'an was used for the text. Anything that advanced Islam was good. Anything that didn't should be avoided. That's the way my father saw the world. At least I always knew where he stood.

I didn't resent my father for saying yes to Arabic calligraphy and no to all other art forms. I didn't fault him for the beating in my bedroom, either. I simply tried harder to live up to my father's strict standards. I adored him too much.

An occasional game of soccer in the courtyard outside our home was my one chance for fun. One day after school I was playing soccer on the playground with twin boys. We got into an argument, and one of the boys popped my soccer ball. It was the ball my father had given me as a gift a few years earlier, the same ball we always used when we'd play together on the sand outside our home.

As the air went out of my ball, I got so mad I cried. Then I punched the boy. His brother jumped to his defense, and I found myself fighting both boys.

That's when my father showed up.

Without asking what had transpired, he beat all three of us.

Then he took me home and announced that I would not be allowed to play soccer until I was sixteen.

That was six years away! I was heartbroken. Soccer was my favorite sport. It was the one game I played with my father. "Please, no, Father," I begged him.

But he held firm. When my father handed down punishment, he was swift, severe, and unforgiving.

Yet my father would stop at nothing to protect me. One afternoon before he suspended my soccer privileges, I was playing on the street in front of our home when a man passed by in a hurry. I inadvertently ran in front of him in an attempt to retrieve my ball. In haste, the man impatiently pushed me aside, causing me to stumble and fall.

The men in our village were outside talking. My father was with them and saw me get knocked down. As I stood and started dusting off my knees, my father charged at the pedestrian and hit him with enough force to knock the man out of his slippers. The man landed in the road. His cap came off, too.

"You dare do that again," my father said, standing over him, "and I will show you."

The man got up, grabbed his cap and slippers, and rushed off.

Despite his small stature, my father had a way of putting fear into other men. No one challenged him. And he was particularly defensive of me.

I was protective of him, too. Scorpions were a big problem in our area. Before putting on our shoes, we always looked inside to make sure one wasn't hiding there. One time my father was in a rush and put his shoes on without checking them. A scorpion stung him, and he was rushed to the hospital. When my cousins heard what had happened, they thought it was funny and started mocking him in front of me.

I slapped one of my cousins across the face. "Open your mouth again, and I will kill you!"

He stopped.

I never let anyone disrespect my father.

I had an uncle with seven sons. Each was named Muhammad. The eldest was Muhammad I, the youngest Muhammad VII. My uncle also had three wives, who were often pregnant at the same time. As a result, three of the Muhammads were born the same year. Those three boys, who were the same age as I was, were always in trouble.

When we were around eleven, one afternoon I heard my three cousins screaming. My uncle, who owned a bicycle shop in the village, was whipping his sons with a bicycle brake cable. He found out they had skipped school the previous day to hang out with hunters who had come into town from the desert to pick up supplies at the local market. They were rough men, unrefined in their dress and coarse in their language. My father and the other men in our mosque had strictly warned us not to associate with the hunters.

"You d-d-didn't go t-t-to school," my uncle shouted as he brought the cable down on his sons repeatedly, making a snapping sound. Because of his speech impediment, he never said much. He just whipped a lot.

I remember the day well because we were all home from school. It was a Friday—our Sabbath—and my father had just returned from a long business trip. As was his custom when he returned from long trips, he invited all of his children and any others who were nearby to gather around him outside. We all knew what that meant—story time. My father was a big believer in the power of oral tradition, and his travels introduced him to all sorts of interesting people and experiences that he passed on to his children. It was his way of trying to inspire and encourage us by blending scripture with tales from his journeys.

We grabbed our mats and surrounded my father on the dusty ground in front of our home. He removed a shiny metal case from his pocket and opened it. "Everybody take one," he said.

Each of us took a white mint and popped it in our mouths. They were pyramid shaped and tasted like peppermint. "They are English mints," my father told us.

When my father saw that his three nephews had welts and dried stripes of blood across their shaved heads, he went in our house and emerged with some iodine and gauze. The sting caused my cousins to cry as my father cleaned and dressed their wounds.

"What they did is not good," my father told us children. "Their father is trying to correct them. That's why he beat them. He doesn't want them to continue skipping school."

We all stared at my cousins' bloodied heads.

"Now," my father said, "I want to tell you a story of a boy whose family thought he had run away."

As soon as he said that, I knew which story he was going to tell. It was one he had shared with me numerous times before, about a teenage boy who disappeared from his family without a trace. The boy's parents searched for him for months in the area surrounding their village in West Africa. After a year of bitter disappointment, the family became convinced that their son had been killed. A funeral was held. Each year on the anniversary of the boy's disappearance, the family held a memorial ceremony in his honor.

This went on for five years. But in truth, the boy had stolen away on a ship that landed him in Liverpool, England. He met some friendly African college students who took him in and helped him gain an education. Then the boy married a white woman from Great Britain. Eventually, he decided to return to his African homeland with his wife.

It was just past the dinner hour when the son entered his family home. His parents were horrified. They thought they were seeing their son's ghost. They cried out in fear as the boy repeatedly told them not to be scared. He insisted he was in fact their missing son. But the scene was so surreal that the parents went into shock.

The son's return touched off commotion in the tiny village.

When things settled down and the parents finally came to grips with the fact that their son was indeed alive, they welcomed him with open arms. The boy apologized profusely and begged forgiveness for the pain and suffering he had caused. He was paraded through the streets as the neighbors sang and cheered his return.

Of the hundreds of tales my father told me over the years, this one stuck with me. Maybe it is because I sensed that it was the one he most wanted me to remember. It spoke to the irresistible force of family bonds and the power of redemption, themes that were strong in Islam and important to my father. He instilled them in me early.

On this particular day, after he finished telling the story, he dismissed all the children except me. Then he said, "If you follow those hunters, you will end up just like the hunters."

I got the message.

Instead of hanging out with my cousins, I stayed close to a group of friends who attended my school. We were in the same classes. We went to the same mosque. Our fathers were friends. There were six of us boys who would come home from school each afternoon and gather under the neem tree across the street from my home. A carpenter was always there in the afternoon, cutting wood on a table. It was like a giant picnic table with benches. We'd sit on the bench and talk while the carpenter worked.

We were learning Shakespeare in school. So we'd often talk about the plays we were reading. My favorite was *Twelfth Night*. But one of my friends loved *Macbeth* and had memorized most of the play. He was always reciting passages from memory.

But one of the boys in my group—his name was Habib—didn't care much for Shakespeare. One day he started calling the rest of us infidels for liking Shakespeare. It was all in good fun. His point was that real men don't get wrapped up in silly sonnets about love. But the nickname stuck. The five of us who read Shakespeare were jokingly referred to as the infidels.

One day the group of us ventured away from our regular spot

and wandered down to the river that was more than a mile from our neighborhood. We passed an area where prostitutes and alcoholics would hang out. Habib, the one who nicknamed us infidels, sneaked up behind two prostitutes who were standing with their backs to us. We didn't know what Habib was up to, and the prostitutes didn't hear him coming. Habib was the biggest boy in our group. He had very large bones and strong hands. With all his might, he hit one of the women over the head with his fist. Her legs collapsed, and she fell to the ground face first.

We all ran toward home. Habib was fanatical like that. He just acted on impulse. But none of us thought twice about the fact that he could have seriously injured a complete stranger. Prostitutes did not deserve mercy.

CHAPTER 3

A YEAR TO REMEMBER

There was an animal market about a mile from our compound. Once a week, on Wednesdays, cowboys from Niger and Chad and all over would gather to sell and trade camels, cows, rams, goats, and sheep. Artisans would sell oils, perfumes, food, cola nuts, breads, and fruits. A huge tamarind tree in the center of the market had a big beehive in it, which was unknown to the men who frequently congregated under it during the market.

One day a perfume trader set up under the tree. When customers approached, he would spray the perfumes for them to sample. One of his perfumes irritated the bees, which emerged from the tree and started stinging people and nearby animals.

The people and the animals started running. Cows and camels broke through their pens. Within moments, thousands of animals were stampeding through the market and into the streets. I was in school that day, and all of a sudden our rooms were locked down. We were told not to leave the school until further notice.

Before the dust settled, a dozen people had been killed and hundreds were hospitalized. Countless animals were stomped to death. It was the worst natural disaster in our village. And it started with the puff of a perfume bottle.

One afternoon not long after the incident at the market, I went home from school for lunch and discovered several cars parked in front of our compound. I didn't recognize any of them. I figured the imam had some visitors from out of town. He and my father were standing outside, between the mosque and our home, talking with a group of men.

Approaching the house, I saw that it was packed with women. Some were chanting. Others were holding their noses and making the sound of a cuckoo bird, long and steady.

Confused, I entered and went looking for my mother. There were containers of cola nuts everywhere. I had never seen so many cola nuts.

"What's going on?" I asked my mother. "Who are all these people?"

"They are from the capital. They are taking your sister Amina."

"What do you mean they are taking Amina?"

"They brought a husband for her."

"What?"

Choking back tears, my mother turned and went into her bedroom.

Amina was fourteen then, four years older than I was. I was my mother's first son. But Amina was her first baby, and without consulting my mother, my father had arranged for her to be married. He had a wealthy business associate who was the biggest distributor of cola nuts in northern Nigeria. He owned massive cola nut farms that were maintained by his sons. One of his sons was in his thirties and had never married, a situation that disappointed the father.

My father offered to fix the problem. "We have a daughter for you," he told the man.

Men were always arranging marriages, but usually the couples at least knew each other. In this instance, the groom-to-be lived more than two hundred miles away in a city called Maiduguri. He'd never seen my sister. Not even a picture of her. My father vouched for her virginity and her beauty. My mother and my sister were not informed until the day before a caravan of strangers arrived at our home to collect my sister. They walked in, and my father presented my sister. It was like going to a market and picking out a new shirt.

That night our family hosted a feast. The men in our neighborhood slaughtered a cow, a ram, and some chickens. My mother and my aunts cooked. The party went late into the evening.

The following morning, my mother put on a brand-new white gown and matching headscarf that my father had purchased for the occasion. He gave her new jewelry to wear, too. But none of it mattered to her. She couldn't stop crying. Conversely, the women from the groom's family were euphoric, dancing around our house, chanting and sounding like geese by holding their noses and honking. That was their way of celebrating.

Early in the morning, immediately after morning prayer, our imam performed the marriage rituals in the mosque. No women are allowed to witness the rituals. Even my sister couldn't attend her own wedding ceremony, since women are not permitted in the mosque and weddings are the business of men. My father represented my sister during the rituals.

After the rituals, my father, in keeping with custom and Islamic law, found my sister and informed her that the wedding had taken place. He handed my sister sweets and cola nuts.

The remainder of the day was spent celebrating. There were feasts and religious music and visitors from all over town. Late in the afternoon, my sister joined her husband for the long journey to her new home. My mother pulled me aside.

"Go and get ready. You are going with them," she told me.

"Why? Aren't you going?"

"No. My sister will be there to help. But I want you to go too."

I went and packed a bag.

I had never been away from home. But I was excited to go. My sister was moving to Maiduguri, the biggest city in the state. It took us all day to drive from our home to Maiduguri. We drove through the night. My sister cried most of the way. After we arrived, my sister and her husband went into the bedroom. By tradition, the bed was prepared with fresh white sheets. This was intentional. After a couple has intercourse for the first time, the white sheets are collected by the groom's mother. The presence of blood stains would prove that my sister was a virgin.

The next morning when I saw her I knew she was no longer a virgin. I had never seen her so sad. Her head was down, her eyes swollen and red. She seemed so far away. I barely recognized her.

"Peace upon you," I said to her.

She did not look up.

Three weeks later, I returned home from Maiduguri. I felt guilty saying good-bye to my sister. She was miserable and homesick. But I was thrilled to go home. My second night back, I walked into town with five or six of my friends. It was sort of a reward—getting to leave the compound with my friends—for spending three weeks helping my sister.

While in town, we walked past the movie cinema. It was behind a high, cinder block wall. In front, vendors sold food, beads, cigarettes, cola nuts, and other items. We stopped to buy some fruit and sugar cane. While snacking, we noticed the movie posters. The depiction of cowboys and Indians attracted us to have a closer look.

I had passed by that movie house plenty of times with my father and other adults from my neighborhood. But I had never looked at the posters. I just knew—all boys from our neighborhood knew—to look the other way. Afraid I was doing something forbidden, I looked over my shoulder to make sure there wasn't anyone around that might recognize me.

"Let's go inside," one of my friends said.

I was the only one with any money. My sister and her new husband had given me a lot of money as a gift when I left them.

The group looked to me. "Buy us tickets," one of them said to me. "Let's go in."

"Are you crazy?" I said. "Somebody could see us."

"We don't have to stay long," one of them said. "Let's just see what it looks like in there."

"Look, I will give you the money," I said. "But I want to go home."

"No. Either all of us go or none of us."

The idea frightened me. I had been taught that only bad people went to the theater and that men went there to pick up prostitutes. Going to a place like that went against all of my beliefs. Just standing outside the door made me nervous. *What if someone I knew walked by and recognized me?*

I'm not sure what got into me. But I finally gave in.

I handed my friend the money. "Here, you buy the tickets."

We approached the ticket window.

Then we entered through a gate. The place was huge. The floor was sand. Lots of people were seated there. There was also a mezzanine level with chairs and a third level with stadium seating. There was no roof. It was more like an outdoor arena. We walked to the mezzanine level and took our seats. People were talking, smoking, and drinking while Indian music played through a sound system. I hated it.

It was about 8:30 at night when coming attractions appeared on the screen. The first one was an Indian movie featuring a belly dancer. The men in the theater shouted and screamed. I looked away.

"Enough," I said to my friends. "Let's go."

39

Some of the boys agreed with me. But two insisted on staying longer.

When the feature film started, I got particularly anxious. The main actor was shooting everybody in sight. At one point, he turned the gun in the direction of the audience. It scared me. I'd never had a gun pointed at me.

"Let's go," I told the others again. "We're going to be late."

This time the boys got up and followed me out.

When we got back to our neighborhood that night, my father was sitting on the stoop in front of my house, waiting for me. I said good night to my friends and approached my front door. Without saying a word, my father stood up and knocked me to the ground with a slap to the face.

Before I could get up, my father had reached for a long stick and started beating me with it. "You come back from the big city and think you can spoil the children around here?" he said.

I wanted to explain that it wasn't my idea. But that would have only made matters worse. Instead, I ran, and he gave chase. I had never run from my father before. But I discovered I was faster. Because of his limp, it took me only a few strides to put distance between us. I ran until I was out of breath. By that time, I looked over my shoulder in the dark and couldn't see anything. Eventually, I walked back toward our house. My father was nowhere around. But I was afraid to go inside. That night I slept under my favorite neem tree across from our house.

Before sunrise, a man walked past the tree on his way to morning prayer at the mosque. "What are you doing here, boy?"

I made up some excuse.

He led me to the mosque for morning prayer. I felt unworthy to go. I knew I had sinned by going to the cinema. I had offended Allah and disgraced my father. Usually, I knelt beside my father at the mosque. This time I hid in the back, where I wouldn't have to face him or the imam. Plus, I didn't want anyone to see the large bruise on my face.

There was no school that day, so I hung around the mosque long after the men left. I pretended to be reading my Qur'an. It was my way of trying to hide my guilt and show my discipleship. But I couldn't focus on the words. In the back of my mind I couldn't help fearing that I might be hauled before a tribunal.

Around mid-morning the door to the mosque opened, and one of my uncles entered. He waved for me to follow him. I figured he had a chore he wanted me to do. Instead, he led me to the imam, who was seated on the veranda with my father and some other men.

I removed my cap and put my face to the ground at his feet. He placed his hands on my head for a moment. Then I sat, facing him.

"How are you?" he asked.

"Thank Allah," I said.

"How is your sister Amina?"

"Thank Allah."

"She was a great woman of good standing. We are all happy for her."

I nodded.

"What is this I hear about last night?"

"I'm sorry."

"How can you go to a cinema?"

"I'm sorry."

"It is one of the most evil places to be. Allah created human beings. Only Allah has the power to create. The cinema has moving pictures. They show evil things. People killing one another."

"They show *women* on the screen!" one of the men shouted.

"And *drinking* and *smoking*," said another. "They show killing and robberies."

I knew these things were evil. The Muslim men who attended our mosque never drank, smoked, gambled, danced, or listened to music. They strictly followed the laws of Islam, which included avoiding the cinema.

"Bad people go there," the imam warned.

I nodded.

"There are prostitutes in the theater," another man said. "Men go there to find them."

"People smoke in there," insisted another.

"Nobody from this community goes to the cinema," the imam said. "You of all people should know."

"I'm sorry."

"We thought when you went away with your sister that you would learn from her. Instead, you went to the city and learned bad things, and you've come back and planted them in the minds of our children. You can't do that."

My father didn't say a word. But he was boiling with anger. My actions had brought shame on him.

"I understand that your sister gave you money to bring home," the imam continued.

I nodded.

"You must not spend it on evil things like cinema," the imam said.

Finally my father spoke. "Western civilization is *eeevil*," he seethed, bringing his fingertips together to form a point as he shook his hand. "Everything Westerners do is evil. *Ev . . . ree . . . thing!*"

I nodded my head.

"They are obsessed with sex. They dress immodestly. Their books and their music and their films are filled with lust and adultery and greed and killing."

Spit flew out of his mouth as he yelled.

"Allah is a God of wrath," he continued. "Jihad is to preserve, to strive, to convince people out of doing bad things. Eventually, *ev . . . ree . . . one* must be converted to Islam. *Jee . . . hadd* is the struggle to bring the world to Allah!"

My father was out of breath.

"Jihad," the imam chimed in, "is to use your own money to get people not to do bad things, to wipe out evil."

"Yes," I said.

"Now you need to ask Allah to forgive you," he said. "You have to pray seriously."

Just then, one of the wealthiest men in our community pulled up in his car. The minute the imam spotted him, he cut off the discussion about my trip to the cinema. "Okay, you try to be a good boy," he said. "Go now. We have visitors."

All eyes were on the rich man as he approached. I grabbed my Qur'an and disappeared unnoticed. Famished, I went home and directly to the kitchen area. My mother was preparing a big pot of okra stew. As soon as she saw the big welt above my eye and the black and blue bruises on my face, she put down her ladle.

"Come," she said, leading me inside. She applied some menthol ointment to the bruises. "You are getting to be a stubborn boy."

It felt like everyone was against me. And nobody understood what really had happened. "We were just playing around," I told my mother. "We found ourselves in front of the cinema, and we just went in. It was like a joke."

"*You* need to be careful," she whispered. "If others do that, it will be overlooked. But you are expected to be different. You cannot go into such places. Never."

CHAPTER 4

GOOD-BYE

My father met all kinds of people on his business trips. And he maintained a vast network of Muslim contacts. Just before my fourteenth birthday he returned from a trip to Maiduguri, where my sister lived. "They are opening an Islamic school there," he began.

Right away I wondered who *they* were. But he didn't say, and I didn't ask.

"You will learn in Arabic and English," he continued. "And it won't be like here, where you go to one school in the morning and another in the evening. You will take religion classes and secular classes in the same place."

That's how I found out I was leaving home for a boarding school. He was talking fast and using his hands to emphasize his words. When he talked like that, his mind was made up.

My mother objected. She didn't want me going two hundred miles away in Nigeria for prep school. Up to that point I had never traveled anywhere, other than when I accompanied my older sister to her new home. In fact, except for that journey, I had never spent as much as a night away from home. She pleaded that it wasn't necessary for me to leave home for school.

But my father brushed aside her reservations and handed me a piece of paper that had been torn from a pad. On it he'd handwritten the school's address. "That's where you apply," he said. "So tell your friends and give them the address. I will make sure you get admitted."

I tucked the paper into my pocket.

"After this school, you'll be able to go to college and study Islam in Mecca or at al-Azhar in Cairo," he said.

That was that. It was settled. I was leaving home for boarding school.

Four months later I entered El-Kanemi College of Islamic Theology. It wasn't a college in the American sense of the word. It was an elite prep school for Muslims desiring to get into one of the top colleges offering degrees in Islamic studies. All of the instructors were Arabs, primarily from Syria. Classes were taught in Arabic. But English classes were also offered.

El-Kanemi's primary financial backer was a Syrian businessman with extensive holdings in Nigeria. In addition to being the sole agent for Toshiba and Akai in Nigeria, he controlled most of the major construction contracts for roads, schools, and hospitals in our country. My father made friends with him and secured his assurance that if I did well at El-Kanemi, he'd help get me admitted to a top Islamic college abroad. This was very important to my father because the secondary schools in Nigeria were woefully underfunded.

While I was in boarding school, I spent my summers back home, working as an understudy to the imam. Usually I was with him while he sat in private, counseling with followers who were struggling with illness, financial loss, family problems, and depression.

In theory, these sessions were religious. But a lot of politics was involved.

One afternoon around 2 p.m. the imam left the mosque just after the midday prayer and took his place on the veranda out front. I was seated on a mat beside him, my back against the porch wall and a writing tablet in my lap. I was writing verses from the Qur'an when a car pulled up. That got my attention. Most men in our neighborhood couldn't afford cars, and driving was forbidden for women, at least for those who were Muslims.

A man in his early forties got out and approached the imam. After removing his shoes and bowing, he said, "I want to talk to you."

The imam stood and motioned for the man to follow him to his parlor. Inside, the man explained his dilemma. He had three wives, but he was attempting to marry a fourth. The girl he wanted to marry was beautiful and belonged to a beautiful family. She was just fourteen. In this situation, custom required the man to take a gift to the girl's father. This is called a token of affection. By accepting the gift, the father consents to the marriage.

But in this case, the man had taken gifts to the father on three occasions—a suitcase full of clothing, a collection of fancy perfumes, and an array of jewelry. All three times the father rejected the gifts.

"I want to try a fourth time," the man told the imam. "What do you say?"

"I will see," the imam said. He reached for a silver serving tray with white sand on it. First he leveled the sand with his hand. Then, using his index finger, he wrote numbers.

The man sat patiently, waiting.

"What's the girl's father's name?" the imam asked.

"Al Haji Abrahim."

The imam nodded. He knew the man, a businessman in the area with multiple wives. "What's the girl's mother's name?"

"Larabe."

The imam grimaced. "You may have a chance," he told the man. "But the mother of the girl is the problem."

"I must marry the girl," the man said. "I must."

The imam nodded. "I will do something about the situation," he said. "The mother's mind must be turned in your favor."

He handed a tablet to the man. "You will do writing on the slate," the imam continued. "Every morning for one week. Then you will wash off the words into a small basin of water. Then you will drink the water."

The man nodded.

"You must sleep on your right hand for one week," the imam continued. "And you must wear this around your neck." He handed him a locket that contained a verse from the Qur'an, compactly folded to the size of a thumbnail. The man attached the locket to a thin rope around his neck.

"Do not remove that locket from your body for a full week," the imam instructed. "Even when you bathe. Then on Friday morning, you bring me a white female goat and a male calf. By then, the family will be ready to release their daughter."

Smiling, the man stood, reached into his pocket, removed a fistful of cash, and placed it under the imam's pillow.

The benefit of having followers who had problems and money is that the imam could obtain things of value like goats and cows in exchange for solving problems. The meat from those two animals would feed the imam, his many wives and children, and the imam's disciples for a couple of weeks. And the status associated with being an imam enabled him to solve problems by asserting his authority.

A few days later, the father of the fourteen-year-old girl arrived to see the imam about a private matter of his own. The imam took him into his parlor and invited him to sit. "How is your daughter?" the imam asked.

"Fine," the man said, caught off guard by the inquiry.

"I learned that there's a man who wants to marry her."

"Ah, yes."

"You object?"

"No. Her mother objects."

"When does the woman in our society have a say in men's affairs?" the imam asked.

The father nodded.

The imam leaned forward and smiled. "Now, when will we be eating her cola nuts?" That was his way of telling the man that there would be a wedding.

The father had no choice but to go along with the imam's wishes. A few days later the imam received his goat and cow from the groom. The wedding was held a week later.

For the first couple of years after my father forbade me to play soccer, I strictly obeyed the restriction. But by the time I was twelve or thirteen, I started occasionally kicking a ball when he was away on business, though I never tried it when he was in town.

Our Egyptian neighbor had a couple of children. They were younger than I was and liked to play soccer. One day a miniature soccer ball sailed over the high wall that separated our home from the Egyptian man's home. The ball rolled to a stop right in front of me.

Instinctively, I dribbled the ball with my foot. I couldn't resist. Then I kicked it a couple of times against the wall.

Next thing I knew, my father was in my face. "I thought I told you not to do that?"

I was frightened. Some years had passed since he had imposed the restriction against kicking a soccer ball. Yet he hadn't forgotten.

"Where did you get the ball?" he asked.

"It just came over the wall."

He grabbed my ear and led me into the house. With my mother looking on, he grabbed a large wooden ruler and told me to lift my shirt. Then he repeatedly struck my back. The beating left stripes.

That was the last time I touched a soccer ball until I moved out of the house. And it was the first time I felt resentment toward my father.

Our divide would ultimately become great. But it started over a soccer ball.

CHAPTER 5

ACCEPTANCE

I was almost seventeen years old when I finished my final semester at El-Kanemi and returned home in the summer of 1977 to await my final exam grades and begin applying to colleges. I had developed into a six-foot-tall teenager with a lean, muscular physique and a serious, purposeful approach to life. Yet I couldn't stop worrying about my grades and whether they'd be high enough for me to gain admittance to a good college. If, for whatever reason, I didn't get an advanced degree in Islamic studies, my father would see me as a complete failure and he'd have grounds to disown me. That kind of pressure made it impossible for me to focus on anything other than fretting about receiving word from my prep school.

I'd been home a couple of weeks when an eight-year-old boy who lived in our village burst into our home, out of breath. "There's a messenger outside," the boy said. "He has a letter for you."

I immediately felt anxious. "Tell him to give it to you," I said.

"No, the man said for you to come quick. This is a very important letter. He needs his cola nuts."

Cola nuts? For a letter? Normally, messengers were not tipped or given gifts for delivering mail. I headed outside.

On the street in front of the house I found a man in trousers wearing a gray gown, sandals, and a cap. He had a canvas satchel over his shoulder and was straddling a bicycle with an oversized rack on the back that was full of parcels and small packages.

"You have a letter for me?" I asked.

"Yes."

"Why didn't you give it to the boy?"

"For this one you have to give me cola nuts."

He had the letter in his hand. I could see that the envelope was unsealed. Clearly, he knew the contents.

"Are you a tax collector?" I said sarcastically.

He smiled. "For today, yes."

"Let me see the letter."

"My cola nuts first. And something from your heart."

Something from your heart? That meant money. This messenger wanted nuts *and* money.

My heart started racing. He had to be delivering good news from my prep school. I ran back in the house and found the cola nuts. Thanks to my sister being married to a grower, we had plenty on hand. Then I went to my mother. "I need some money," I told her.

"How much?"

"Ten shillings."

I walked back outside and handed the messenger a jar of nuts and the coins, and he handed me the letter. I started reading:

"I am pleased to inform you that you have been accepted to the Furquan Institute in Damascus, Syria."

I snapped my eyes back to read the first line again. Then I read the instructions to apply for a passport and complete a physical exam in preparation for traveling to Syria as a student.

"God is great!" I shouted. "I've been accepted! I've been accepted!"

I waved the letter over my head and started jumping in the street. The men who were sitting on the veranda listening to the imam came running. "What is going on?" they demanded.

I showed them the letter. "I'm going to Damascus!" I shouted.

The men surrounded me and started jumping and chanting. "Allah is great. Allah is great. Allah is great."

Before I knew it, I was on their shoulders. All the commotion drew my mother to the front door just in time to see me being paraded down the street toward the iman, who was waiting on the veranda outside the mosque. My mother, who was prohibited from coming out to the street, peeped through the partially open doorway, trying to ascertain what was happening. Other women in the compound started looking through windows, too.

The men who carried me down the street sang the fourteen-hundred-year-old song that Ansar had sung to the prophet Muhammad upon his arrival at Medina after fleeing Mecca:

> Oh the white moon rose over us
> From the valley of al-Wada
> And we owe it to show gratefulness
> Where the call is to Allah
> Oh you who were raised among us
> Coming with a word to be obeyed
> You have brought to this city nobleness
> Welcome best caller to God's way.

From atop the men's shoulders, I wished my father were back from his business trip to see all the fuss. It would have made him proud to see me treated like a hero.

The men put me down in front of the imam.

"Be seated," he said to me, smiling.

I took my place on the deck of the veranda. Dozens of men formed a half circle behind me.

"What is the good news?" he asked.

"I received this letter."

He extended his hand, and I gave it to him. A smile swept across the imam's face as he read it to himself.

"Thanks to Allah!" he shouted, raising his hands toward heaven.

"There is no God but Allah," the men responded in unison.

"Where is the man who brought the news?" the imam asked.

One of the imam's disciples pointed to the street. "He is standing by the bicycle," the disciple said.

"Bring him forward," the imam said.

The men behind me parted, creating a pathway for the messenger to approach. He put down his kickstand, dropped his bag, removed his sandals, and approached and knelt before the imam, who extended his right hand. The messenger clasped the imam's hand in his hands and then wiped his palms against his own chest, passing blessings from the imam to himself.

The imam reached under his pillow and removed a wad of money.

The messenger cupped his hands, and the imam placed the money in them.

"Thank you," the messenger said, bowing and turning toward his bicycle. He was about to ride off when the imam cleared his throat.

"Do you have other letters like this one?" the imam called out, waving mine in his hand.

Straddling his bicycle, the messenger looked over his shoulder. "Yes."

"Bring them," the imam said, waving him back.

The messenger rifled through his bag, selecting five more letters.

Before he took a step, the imam's disciples snatched them from his hand and ran with them to the imam. He flipped through them. Spotting one addressed to his son Buba, he opened it and began reading.

"Allah is great," he shouted, raising his hands to heaven. "Allah is great. Allah is great."

We all repeated those words three times.

"Bring my son to me at once," the imam boomed. "And bring the other boys, too."

It was clear that Buba and the others had received acceptance letters too. A couple of the imam's disciples ran off to retrieve the boys. The rest of the audience sat down on the ground in front of the imam. Only the carrier remained standing. Seeing him, the imam reached back under his pillow and pulled out a much bigger handful of money. One of the disciples took it to the carrier. "Today is your day," he told him.

Elated, the carrier rode off with a pouch full of money while the imam rushed into his chamber and emerged moments later with a tub of toffee. He gave me a handful. Then he handed the tub to his disciple, who shared the candy with everyone.

The imam went back to his chamber and brought out more candy. "Take this to the woman," he instructed another of his disciples.

I knew that meant the imam was sending candy to my mother.

Moments later the imam's son came running, along with one of my cousins. They took their seats beside me. Everyone grew quiet.

"You have done well," the imam said, looking at the three of us. "I am very happy that you raised the name of Nguru high. And I really want you to study seriously when you go to Damascus."

He motioned me to step forward first.

I removed my cap, and he placed his right hand on my forehead. "In the name of Allah, Most Gracious, Most Merciful," he began. "Praise be to Allah, the Cherisher and Sustainer of the Worlds.

Most Gracious, Most Merciful; Master of the Day of Judgment; Thee do we worship, and Thine Aid we seek. Show us the straight way, the way of those on whom Thou has bestowed Thy Grace, those whose portion is not wrath. And who go not astray. Amen."

"Amen," I said.

He repeated the same prayer for his son and my cousin. Then he raised his arms high above his head and looked up. "In the name of Allah," he prayed.

We raised our hands and repeated his words.

It was a highlight of my adolescent years to be the subject of so much praise.

An hour passed before the imam released us. I went directly home. My mother was still waiting by the door.

"A letter came that said I'm going to Syria," I told her.

She tilted her head, and the skin above her brow bunched up. "Where?"

"Syria."

"For how long?"

"At least four years."

"What?"

"Yes, we are going to study."

"No. Not you. The other boys can go. But not you."

"I need to go. It is very good for me. I need to get a higher education."

"You can do it here," she insisted.

I just looked at her.

"Where did the imam go to study?" she asked. "He went to Mecca to pray and then came back here to study. He didn't go abroad."

I still said nothing.

"So the other boys can go. But you cannot. I will not allow it."

"Father wants me to go," I said.

"He can send his other sons, but not you. You are my only son."

Crying, I walked away.

Three days later my father returned from his business trip. He went straight to the mosque. When I arrived, he and the imam were seated on the floor, facing each other, inside the imam's chambers.

"I have arranged for you and the other boys to get passports and see a doctor in the capital," my father told me.

I nodded.

"We are leaving in the morning," he said.

Normally, passports take months to secure in Nigeria. My father wanted to speed up the process by going directly to the ministry where passports are processed.

"Go find the other boys and tell them to prepare to leave," my father told me.

I bowed to the imam and ran out, hardly able to wait to get my passport. The rest of my day was spent tracking down the other boys from the village who were going to Damascus and attending the afternoon and evening prayers. That night my mother cornered me in my room. By that time my father had told her the plan.

"So you want to go?" she said.

"What can I do? Father said I have to go. The imam said I have to go."

Dropping her chin to her chest, she turned and walked out.

Torn, I just stood there. I liked pleasing my father, but I hated seeing my mother so sad. Her expression drained the enthusiasm right out of me.

It took three months for our passports and other paperwork to come through. On my last day at home, the imam called a special evening prayer service at the mosque for the three of us who were going to Damascus. He kept us there until nearly 11 p.m. Then I went directly to bed. But I couldn't sleep. A thin wall separated my room from my parents' room. I could hear them arguing.

"He's too young to go that far away," she said. "We have no relatives there."

"In Syria he will have the best teachers," my father argued.

"The teachers at the boarding school in Maiduguri are all Syrians. So why does he have to go all the way to Syria? Why can't he continue studying in Maiduguri?"

It was the first time I had heard my mother voice her opinion. Outspoken women were wicked women. Obedient women never argued with their husbands. Questioning your husband was grounds for a severe beating. The more she questioned the more scared I became for her safety.

"Why?" she continued. "Tell me."

"Enough!"

"I see no reason."

"He is finished here! He'll get a higher education there. Now enough, woman!"

"Is it not enough, all the time he has spent in school already? Now he has to go far?"

Her words just hung there. My father never responded. The next thing I heard was my mother whimpering. She cried herself to sleep that night. So did I.

I felt groggy when my father woke me up for morning prayer. I'd been attending morning prayer with him for eleven years. But on this occasion I felt different. Kneeling beside him, I felt I had reached a milestone in the quest to becoming a spiritual leader. He didn't say anything that morning. He didn't have to. His proud glance warmed me like a fire. For a boy, there's nothing like the satisfaction that comes from making his father proud.

After prayer, the imam pulled his son and me into his chamber. He had a slate with words written in chalk. He washed the slate clean, collecting the chalky water in a cup. After adding a touch of honey, he handed me the cup.

"This is for knowledge," he said. "Whatever you read cannot be forgotten."

I drank from the cup. Even honey couldn't mask the bitter taste.

I handed the cup to my cousin, and he finished it off. Then his father handed each of us a locket on a leather string. "Put it around your neck," he said.

We did as instructed.

"Now, put this inside," he said, handing me a piece of paper folded to the size of a postage stamp. It contained instructions on how to pray, how often to read, and which scriptures to read in the morning, at midday, and at night. "Never remove the locket from your neck. Never. Even when you wash."

I bowed and turned to leave his chamber.

"You have to step out with your left foot," he told me.

I stopped. In Islam we always step out of rooms with our right foot first. Always.

"When you go out with your left foot," the imam explained, "no matter what may happen to you in Syria, you will return here."

I led with my left. Then I hurried home to say good-bye to my mother. I found her in the house. Her eyes were bloodshot, and her lips were quivering. Her brother Isa was standing beside her. He lived a few miles away and had come to see me off.

"Here," Isa said, handing me a fistful of Egyptian pounds. "Hide this. You may need it."

I slid the bills in a pocket that my father had sewn into the binding of my Qur'an.

"Your bags are in the car," Isa told me.

My father was waiting outside for me.

I wanted to put my arms around my mother. But physical affection was discouraged in our culture. "Good-bye," I said meekly.

She lifted her hand, waving slowly with her fingers.

"It's time to go," my father called.

"C'mon," Isa said.

I turned and headed for the door.

My mother sobbed.

I turned and ran to her. I knelt down and hugged her legs. I could feel her tears hitting the top of my head.

"It's time, woman," my father yelled.

"Let's go," my uncle said, pulling me away. "Let's go."

"Good-bye, Hauwa," I whispered.

"Good-bye," she mouthed.

Tears ran down my cheeks.

She followed me to the door. But she couldn't pass the threshold and accompany me to the car. That was another one of the customs of our imam. She wailed as I got into the car.

My father drove the van to the regional airport in Kano. The 250-mile journey gave me time to think. That wasn't a good thing. I started having second thoughts about going away. But my father buoyed me. By the time we reached the airport, I was somber but steadfast. We would meet again, he told me. Until then, he said, Allah would look down on me and bless me for my dedication to the faith.

"You are ready," he said. "You are ready."

There was no warm embrace. No pat on the back. No words of love. Saying good-bye to my father was more like saluting.

CHAPTER 6

THE ROAD TO DAMASCUS

It was late afternoon by the time my flight left Nigeria. The minute I was airborne I looked down toward the direction of home. I hoped to see lights from that area. I thought that would draw me closer to my mother. But the distance was too great. Even from twenty thousand feet I couldn't see my homeland.

I already felt like my mother was far away. It felt like I might never see her again. Depressed, I started reciting verses from the Qur'an in hopes of lifting my spirits. It worked. Somehow, the passages I had memorized as a boy soothed me. Maybe it was the familiarity.

We touched down in Cairo at nighttime. Our connecting flight to Damascus didn't depart until the following morning. We were scheduled to spend the night at a hotel near the airport. I was homesick. But my mind quickly shifted from sadness to shock the moment I stepped off the plane and entered the airport terminal in Cairo. For the first time I saw the faces of Arab women. They weren't wearing veils, scarves, or caps. Worse, they were dressed in tight-fitting jeans and T-shirts that exposed their arms. I had no idea that Arab women dressed that way. Why, I wondered, weren't the Arab women in Cairo following the same Islamic rules as the Muslim women in Nigeria?

Arab men were dressed differently too. They wore open-collar shirts, for one thing. Chest hair was visible. Back home, an Arab man would be ashamed to dress that way. I would have been beaten for wearing anything other than the traditional garb. Yet the airport was full of informally dressed Arabs.

I wasn't sure whether to be angry or nervous. The whole scene was just so foreign to me.

We collected our luggage and went to a mosque that our fathers told us was located beneath the main level of the airport. We intended to pray before going to our hotel for the night.

In accordance with Islamic law, we attempted to practice the rituals of ablution before entering the mosque. We were about to wash our faces, hands, and feet when an Arab man stepped between the fountain and us. He extended his arm, the palm of his hand facing up. Clearly he wanted something.

"What?" I asked.

"Baksheesh," the man said, rubbing the tips of his fingers with his thumb. In Arabic, baksheesh means "tip."

"For what?" I said.

"For ablution," he said.

"We pay for ablution?"

"Yes."

"I have to pay before I pray?"

"Yes."

I turned to my companions. "Do you hear what this man says? He's asking us to pay."

"We better go along," one of them said.

61

"No. In the Arab world I have to pay to pray? I can't do that."

The man in front of the fountain gave us a dirty look.

"I won't do it," I repeated.

"You have to," one of my friends whispered.

I turned to the man. "Where we come from, every man has to put his vase of water outside to wash before he enters the mosque to pray," I told him. "You want me to pay money to pray. I won't do it."

He folded his arms across his chest and scowled at me. The other boys reached into their pockets, removed money, and handed it to him. He let them wash and enter. I remained outside.

That experience and the way Arabs were dressed in the airport convinced me that Cairo was a corrupt place.

When we arrived in Syria the following day, things got even stranger. Leaving the airport terminal, I saw all the Arab men from my plane embracing and kissing Arab men who were there to greet them. I had never seen a man kiss a man. I turned to my cousin. "Hey, what is going on here?" I whispered.

He shrugged his shoulders.

Then I spotted a young-looking, very dark African man with a giant Afro. He had on jeans and a tight-fitting leather jacket that showcased his muscular upper body. When I made eye contact with him, he flashed a big smile and kept staring at me. It made me nervous. He was built like a football player, and from his clothing I guessed he wasn't a Muslim.

The man next to him was looking at me too. He was only about five-foot-eight. But he had to weigh more than three hundred pounds. His stomach was massive. No one back home was that fat. But at least I knew he was a Muslim. He had on the traditional robes.

Finally, the African man stepped toward us and extended his hand. "Hello. My name is Chuks."

Instantly I knew he was Christian. Chuks (Chooks) is a tribal name with Christian roots from eastern Nigeria. Plus, he was speaking in English, not Arabic.

I froze. So did my cousins.

"I am a fellow Nigerian," Chuks continued, still smiling. "I'm a student at the institute, and I'm here to escort you back."

Confused, I quickly glanced at my cousins. We were thinking the same thing: *Why was a Christian student at an Islamic institute?*

"And this is Professor Yusuf," Chuks said, pointing to the fat man in robes. "He is the head of the hostel where you'll be staying."

"Welcome," Yusuf said in a deep voice, reaching for my hand.

Relieved, I extended my hand. "I am Muhammad. These are my cousins."

"I hope you boys learn well at the school," Yusuf said.

"Thank you," I said.

"Now," Chuks said, "you'll need to turn over your passports and traveler's checks to Professor Yusuf."

We reached into our pockets.

"And if you have any money for safekeeping you should give that to him, too."

Each of us had eighteen hundred dollars in traveler's checks. We handed them over with our passports. We didn't let on that we had cash.

Chuks and Yusuf then escorted us to collect our luggage from the baggage claim. Uniformed soldiers were all over the terminal. I hadn't seen any soldiers in the Cairo airport and certainly none in Nigeria.

As soon as our luggage was loaded into Yusuf's car, he headed back to campus. Chuks led us to a transit bus. He said he was taking us sightseeing in Damascus before going to the school. I ended up in a seat beside Chuks. I'd never been so close to a Christian. Unsure what to say, I stared out the window. The first thing I noticed were women dressed in green uniforms. They were everywhere.

"Why are these women dressed like they are in the military?" I asked.

"Syria is at war with Israel," Chuks whispered. "So everybody of military age has to serve in the military. Even women."

"What?"

"Yes," he said, nodding his head up and down.

I had no idea that Syria was at war. It was something my father should at least have mentioned.

"Look down that road," Chuks said, pointing out the window. "It leads to Umayyad Mosque. It's the biggest mosque in the world."

I strained to see it.

"You can't see it from here," he said. "But it's where John the Baptist's head is kept in a shrine."

I had no idea what he was talking about. He could tell.

"You know John the Baptist, don't you?" Chuks asked. "The one who baptized Christ?"

"The Qur'an mentions John the Baptist," I said. "But it doesn't say that he baptized Jesus."

"Islam doesn't mention that. But he did."

I nodded.

"That street," he said a little while later, pointing again, "is Straight. It's where Saul was blinded by the light when he saw Christ."

"Who is Saul?"

"Saul is Paul. One of Christ's disciples."

"Back home there was a Christian school called St. Paul's. And I knew some Christians named Paul. But I never knew the significance of the name."

"Paul was one of Christ's disciples," Chuks explained. "But before becoming a disciple, Paul persecuted Christians."

I cocked my head. "Their killer became their leader?"

Chuks smiled. "Well, Christ appeared to him, and he was blinded. That happened here in Damascus, on that street that we

64

just passed. Paul was then taken to some Christian man's house here in the city, and they prayed for him."

It never occurred to me that Damascus had such a rich Christian heritage, particularly since roughly 75 percent of the city's 1.5 million residents are Muslims. I never realized the weather got so cold in Damascus, either. I couldn't stop shivering.

"Here, take my coat," Chuks offered.

"No, thank you. It's okay."

Suddenly the bus stopped. Three guys with machine guns approached the door. They had ammunition belts strapped across their shoulders and chests.

Frightened, I ducked.

"It'll be okay," Chuks whispered.

The armed men entered the bus. "IDs," one of them announced.

I panicked. I had given my passport to Yusuf at the airport. I had no identification. Neither did my cousins.

As the soldier approached, my hands shook uncontrollably.

Chuks showed his ID. Then the soldier looked at my cousins and me.

"They are students," Chuks said in Syrian Arabic. "I just received them from the airport. The principal from the school has their passports."

The soldier nodded and moved on.

I finally exhaled. I wished I could go home. A few minutes later the bus entered an enormous roundabout and pulled to a stop. "We're getting off here," Chuks told us.

We stepped out into a busy bus terminal. People and vehicles were everywhere.

"What is the name of this place?" I asked.

"Al-Marje Square. It's the center of Damascus. This is where they hanged Cohen."

My father had told me about Eli Cohen, the Israeli spy who worked his way into the highest levels of the Syrian government before being discovered and hanged in a high-profile execution in 1965.

"My father used to talk about him," I told Chuks. "We know him by his Arabic name: Kamel Amin Thaabet. My dad called him the million-dollar spy."

"Well, he was executed right there," he said, pointing to a spot not a hundred feet from where we stood.

"Right there?"

"Yes. And they left him hanging there so people could come and see him."

Chuks pivoted and pointed toward a hotel. "That's where three Palestinian terrorists—a girl and two men—were caught trying to carry out an assassination," he said. "The girl was shot by the police. The two men were tied to the back of a jeep and dragged through the streets of Damascus."

I thought to myself, *My mother was right. This is no place for me.*

Yet, walking around Damascus, I couldn't help being fascinated with the architecture of the world's oldest city. I had never seen such impressive buildings. Nothing in Nigeria compared.

Deep down inside, I had aspirations to become an architect. Designing buildings was something I had dreamed about since entering the British primary school at age six. Design went hand in hand with my love for drawing. But my father would never entertain the idea of my doing anything other than joining the clergy.

Nor would my father have fathomed a Christian escorting me around Damascus, talking to me about the city's history with Christianity. He'd see Chuks as a heathen. But I started liking him the moment he offered me his coat. He seemed genuine, kind, smart, and informed—everything my father wanted me to be.

Still, I couldn't figure out why a Christian was enrolled in an exclusively Islamic school. That made no sense to me. Neither did a lot of other things I witnessed in my initial forty-eight hours away from home—Arabs in Egypt dressed like Westerners, clergy outside a Cairo mosque demanding bribes, women in Syria dressed like men and serving in the military. It was quickly becoming apparent just how little I knew about the Arab world outside Nigeria, not to mention the culture and history that had shaped the Muslim faith. Life in my Nigerian village in Nguru had left me naïve about the rest of the world.

By the time we arrived at the campus, I was exhausted. Chuks took us straight to the hostel. It was a large home that had been converted to a boarding house. Yusuf was there, and he led us to our sleeping quarters, a drab, cramped room with beat-up furniture and cot-style beds covered in mismatched linens.

Eager to see the campus, we didn't bother unpacking. We walked a block to the El-Furqan Institute of Islamic Theology, which was surrounded by a high fence. The only way in was through an iron gate. A small administration building and a cafeteria were just inside the fence and then a collection of small classroom buildings, each with bare concrete walls and narrow transom windows up near the ceiling, making it impossible to see out.

I was expecting a college campus. All of us were. But it felt more like a second-rate boarding house. No big buildings with impressive architecture. No courtyard. No dormitories. The private high school I attended in Nigeria was nicer.

The student body was a bit of a shock, too. There were about two hundred students in all. Besides Chuks, only about a dozen were from Africa. Most were from Turkey and Yugoslavia. It wasn't clear to me what all of these non-Muslims were doing at a private Muslim school in Syria.

It got even more confusing on the first day of classes. That's when I discovered that math and science classes weren't offered. Neither were foreign language courses or literature classes. All the courses were tied to Islamic studies, and the Qur'an was the primary text in every class. Did my father know it was going to be like this? I had to wonder.

The other thing that I noticed right away was that all of the teachers shouted when they taught. They weren't really teachers. They were more like religious fanatics. Very angry fanatics.

Yusuf, it turned out, was the most fanatical of all. He was the teacher for a class on the Qur'an. His method of teaching was rote memorization, the same method I had grown up with. So it was pretty easy for me. Boring. But easy. It wasn't so easy, however, for a Turkish boy. He was a bit of a social misfit to begin with. He was a dwarf and had extremely large teeth. The other boys shunned him on account of his physical limitations.

I had been enrolled in school only a few days when Yusuf called on this boy to stand up and recite a lengthy passage from the Qur'an. He got to a point where he forgot the words. So he tried quickly jumping ahead to the next verse.

Yusuf backhanded the boy across the mouth. "May Allah forgive you for this sin," Yusuf said. "You reduced the verses."

With a pointer in his opposite hand, Yusuf faced the rest of us. "You can't take away from or add to the holy verses of the Qur'an."

Scared, the students all nodded.

"In my class, I will always allow anybody to stop," he continued. "When you get to a place where you can't remember, you stop there and say, I can't remember. Never, ever jump to the next verse. That is a sin. And you are invoking Allah's anger over all of us who are listening."

The Turkish dwarf weighed about sixty pounds. Next to Yusuf he looked even smaller. Blood dripped from his mouth. I decided then and there that I didn't like Yusuf.

For the first few weeks at the institute, all our meals were prepared by kitchen staff and served in the cafeteria. Breakfast consisted of milk, bread, cheese, and bean soup. Lunch was rice and beans. Dinners varied.

One evening during dinner hour, Yusuf made an announcement.

"This is your last meal on the school," he said. "Tomorrow you start cooking for yourselves."

Cook? Me? I panicked. Back home, boys were strictly forbidden to cook. I was beaten just for entering the kitchen. Boys who cook never marry. My mother swore by this.

Yusuf assigned us to groups of six, and the staff handed us a set of cookware: one large soup pot, a smaller pot for boiling macaroni and rice, a frying pan, some basic cooking utensils, and a spoon and a fork for eating. We also received a week's supply of staple foods: rice, beans, boxes of macaroni, and cans of tuna fish and sardines. Our pita bread came from a local bakery. We took our things to a cellar beneath the cafeteria, where the kitchen was located. Each group was assigned an oversized wooden cubbyhole in which to store our things.

"Tomorrow," one of the staff told us, "you come here, pick up your things, and cook."

I had trouble sleeping that night. "We're going to *cook* for ourselves?" I kept saying to my cousins. "This is a big problem."

The next day, I bumped into Chuks at mealtime. He saw the anxiety in my eyes. "What's wrong?" he asked.

"I don't know how to cook," I said. "The other guys from my village don't know how, either."

"Don't worry, my brother," Chuks said. "I will teach you how to cook."

Chuks escorted us into the cooking area. We were given access to a small kerosene stove with four burners. It was a big change from the way my mother cooked in clay pots over an open fire. The first thing I had to learn was how to light a stove. Chuks handed me a bellows.

"Pump air into a chamber beneath the burners," he told me. "That pushes the kerosene through."

The fumes irritated my nose and throat.

Chuks smiled. "You'll get used to it."

I pumped the bellows a couple more times. Then I struck a match and tossed it on the burner. A flame shot up. I jumped back. But the flame singed my hair. My burnt hair reminded me of the odor coming from the smoldering hair on the heads of rams sitting by the fire on my mother's cooking veranda back home.

"Next time don't pump so fast," Chuks said. "And never stand over the burner when tossing a match."

The other students laughed. I didn't think it was funny. But before long, Chuks had me boiling water and cooking macaroni and rice. Then I started adding vegetables and making simple meals. I found that I loved cooking my own food.

The only reason I wanted to leave home was to study abroad at a college that offered art and science classes from top professors. I knew I was destined for the clergy. But along the way I thought I'd get a first-rate education in areas other than religion. Instead, I was at an institute with clerics instead of professors. And the whole curriculum was based on the Qur'an and supplemental religious books. Classes quickly became drudgery. At the same time, school rarely let first-year students leave campus. I felt trapped.

I felt cheated, too. I thought back to the argument that took place between my parents the night before my departure. My father had stifled my mother's complaints about me leaving home by pointing out that I had chosen to study in Syria. Well, I certainly hadn't chosen the situation I was in.

I hadn't chosen the harsh conditions of the institute, either. Boys were routinely slapped and beaten for breaking trivial school rules. Something as simple as failing to properly recite a passage of the Qur'an resulted in a beating. The instructors liked to strike boys in the face with an open hand. I knew the Qur'an exceptionally well and therefore never got in trouble for misstating scripture.

But the instructors seemed to go out of their way to find excuses to discipline us. One time a Nigerian student overslept, causing him to be late for class. After beating the boy, the instructor locked the student in a storage room, where he was left for two days. On another occasion, a small group of Turkish students got into trouble for going to the cinema on their day off. Normally, Fridays between 2 p.m. and 7 p.m. were considered free time for students to venture into Damascus and do as they chose. The cinema was a popular venue for the guys at the institute. Arab films were permitted. But when school authorities learned that these boys had watched a Western film, the boys were hauled before the entire student body and beaten.

"My brother," Chuks told me toward the end of my first year at the institute, "these Arabs don't wish us any good. All they want is for us to study Islam and Arabic."

Due to our age difference, we weren't in any classes together. But outside of class we got together to talk in the evenings. When the two of us were alone one night, I asked how he, as a Christian, ended up at an Islamic institute. He informed me that he was raised Christian, but his parents had converted to Islam when he was a teenager. "I never converted," he confided. "Not in my heart. But my father arranged for me to come here."

Chuks was the brightest student at the institute by far. But he wasn't happy. "They won't even let me pay my own way to take some classes at Damascus University," he said.

"What are you telling me? They won't let you go to Damascus to attend other lectures?"

"No way," he said.

"Why not?"

"They will never allow it. Either you do their courses exclusively, or you leave."

"I don't understand."

He looked over his shoulder to make sure no one else was nearby. "Are you familiar with the Muslim Brotherhood?" he whispered.

71

"In Nigeria it means that we are all brothers, that we are our brother's keeper," I said.

"Well, it's different in Syria."

"What do you mean?"

The Brotherhood, he explained, was known more formally as the Society of the Muslim Brothers and was founded in the 1920s in Egypt. It's an Islamic political organization with the primary objective to return Muslims to an orthodox interpretation of Islam by making the Qur'an the single reference point for all aspects of life. Over time the Brotherhood spread throughout the Arab world. Some of its members have an unstated goal to convert non-Muslims to the faith.

"Here the Brotherhood is against the government," he said. "They want a fully Islamic state."

"As a Muslim, I'd love to see an Islamic state," I said.

"My brother, you don't understand. You see how the teachers treat students here?"

"Sure. Harshly."

"Well, a lot of the boys here came from non-Muslim backgrounds, like me," he said. "But their tuition is paid for by a member of the Brotherhood."

"I don't understand."

"They pay for us to go to school here because they want us to return to our home countries as Muslims."

I was starting to get the picture.

"This is a place of indoctrination," he said.

I started to question the motives behind the Syrian businessman who had arranged for my enrollment at the institute. Surely, he had ties to the Brotherhood. But what about my father? I had never heard him say much about them. He had to know about the school's ties to the movement.

I wasn't sure how all of this affected me. But I knew I would not have made it through my first year without Chuks. He became my best friend. He was the only person I trusted. Toward the end of the school year, I dropped by his room and found him packing his bags.

"What are you doing?"

"Packing."

"Why?"

"I'm returning to Nigeria."

"Why?"

"I've been deported."

"Deported?"

He zipped his bag shut. "Sit down, my brother."

I plopped down on his cot, and he explained the situation. He had a Syrian sponsor who was paying his tuition. Suddenly the man had withdrawn support. "His real motive was to indoctrinate me in Islamic fundamentalism, not help me become a scientist or doctor," Chuks said.

"So without his money you can't stay?"

"It's deeper than that. My sponsor and the school are tired of me pushing to take classes elsewhere."

"So they are pushing you out?"

"But you're the best student here. They shouldn't be able to get rid of you that way."

"It's all right, my brother. I want to leave. I've had enough."

He zipped his last bag and smiled at me. "God be with you," he said.

"God be with you," I replied.

CHAPTER 7

RAISING RADICALS

One class in particular was a real struggle for me—Islamic philosophy. The material wasn't particularly challenging. The problem was the teacher. A huge man with thick bones and a gray beard, he was an extremist when it came to convincing students that Allah's existence could be proved through logic. Inquisitive by nature, I started asking questions. That's when trouble started.

One day I put up my finger in class.

"Yes, Momen," he said.

"I have a question."

"Ask."

"I just want to clarify one thing."

"Go ahead," he said, wagging his finger at me. "But I don't want any of your trouble."

"If I have a headache and I take an aspirin and then feel better,

I know it is by the power of Allah. But it is also the aspirin that healed me, no?"

"You are giving power to the aspirin and not to Allah. That is a big sin."

"But—"

"Stop there, Momen. I don't want any more of your trouble. You want to blaspheme. And we don't want to hear those things."

After class I was summoned to the headmaster's office, an elaborately furnished room with polished wood paneling and a pervasive aroma of musk cologne. He was a rich sheik who wore an Italian suit jacket over his gown.

"Please sit down," he said in a friendly tone. He was leaning on a polished cedar walking stick with a silver cap.

Nervous, I sat opposite his desk.

"I heard about your encounter with the teacher," he said, clasping his fingers. They were covered in gold rings, and he had diamond cuffs on his shirtsleeves. "What didn't you understand?"

"I can speak?"

"Yes. Please."

"I understand that Allah is all powerful and puts power into everything, even the food we eat. But if I take aspirin and feel better, I want to know why I can't say that the aspirin made me feel better."

"As Muslims we know that all power belongs to Allah. And only with Allah's permission and power can we do anything. Can you stand up without Allah's power?"

"No. But when I stand up, I say that I stood up. I don't say Allah stood me up."

"You aren't listening. You can't learn."

"Sir, I'm trying to understand."

"No!" he shouted, banging his walking stick on the floor. "You are going to a no-go area."

"Sir, I'm from Africa. In Africa there are many pagans. They don't believe this. I need to convince them with logic. And logically, what you are telling me doesn't make sense to me. So how will it make sense to pagans?"

"Allah's words are not logical to you?" he screamed.

He had a set of religious beads in his hand. He whipped me across the face with them.

"Out!" he screamed. "You want to be an atheist? We know how to deal with you."

That night at dinner I learned my meals had been revoked for a day. I went twenty-four hours without food. That was the first time I was punished at the school.

I wasn't the only boy with questions. But none of the others dared to ask them. Nor did they come to my defense. No one wanted to be labeled an atheist like me. I resented that label. My belief in God was fixed.

Around this time I struck up a friendship with a Yugoslavian student named Yalmaz. He was a closet atheist. At the conclusion of classes each day, Yalmaz would stay behind and write Arabic calligraphy on the chalk board. I started sticking around to watch him. Eventually, Yalmaz offered to teach me calligraphy. That's how our friendship began.

Yalmaz was four years older than I. He had been raised in a Communist country. On the surface we had little in common, except that we were both stuck in some place we didn't like. Yalmaz had ended up at El-Furqan because his father insisted that he go there. He was the first atheist I had ever met. Everyone I had grown up around believed in the Almighty. Even Muslims and Christians agreed on the existence of a God. The concept of a world without a God was one I couldn't fathom.

Yalmaz did not feel the same way. To him it was silly to believe in God. But he didn't try to persuade me to change my beliefs. He never uttered a word about his atheism at the Islamic school, until I came along. When no one was around, we would talk in hushed tones about all sorts of religious topics. No one knew that Yalmaz believed in atheism, not even his parents. They were Muslims and had raised their son to follow Islam. He was just never convinced. But he was afraid to tell his father.

I thought about that and the fact that my relationship with my father was also influenced by fear. Not that this was a new discovery on my part. By the time I hit my teen years I had started to appreciate how much fear dictated my actions around my father. But being around Yalmaz got me analyzing how much that fear influenced my religious beliefs. In other words, were my beliefs based on faith or fear? I wasn't sure.

I knew one thing, though. If my father found out I had befriended an atheist, he would flog me. To ensure that he never found out, I was careful not to tell my stepbrother, my cousins, or any of the boys from back home who were enrolled in the school. Yalmaz wanted it that way, too. He even went as far as to tell me that he'd deny our friendship if I ever spoke of it.

Eventually, Yalmaz told me how much he admired the teachings of Karl Marx. I had been taught that Marx was the biggest infidel of all time. That's what my father believed. Yet I didn't recoil when Yalmaz went on about the virtues of Marxism. I guess that was a sign that I was becoming more tolerant.

Although I didn't agree with Marxism, I found the conversation stimulating and intriguing. These conversations also gave rise to more questions about Islam. It wasn't that my commitment to Islam had changed. Nor was I about to embrace atheism or Marxism. Far from it. It was just that I felt safe to question traditional beliefs and conventional wisdom when I was around Yalmaz.

Meantime, it seemed like my instructors were becoming increasingly radical. Especially Yusuf. In my third year I had him for a class called Hadith. *Hadith* means "Muhammad's traditions." The class was designed to get us to memorize Muhammad's doctrines. His writings were the text.

Yusuf used this class to advance Islamic fundamentalism. The primary theme he kept emphasizing was that Western civilization was evil and therefore had to be rooted out. Most of the rhetoric was directed against Israel. Peace and righteousness, he taught, would not reign on earth until Israel was wiped out.

I had heard plenty of fiery sermons back in Nigeria. But the institute in Damascus was the first place where I had been told that if a Muslim died in the process of killing a nonbeliever, his reward would be a mansion in paradise. This just seemed twisted to me. As an African I had experienced and witnessed plenty of racism from Arabs. This hatred toward Westerners and Jews sounded like more racism. But I never brought that up.

There were other things that I did question, though. One of our booklets had a passage indicating that Muhammad was ordered to kill.

"He was ordered to kill people until they testified that there is no God but Allah," Yusuf told us.

I put up my finger.

"Yes?"

"I have a question."

"Ask."

"There is no subject in that sentence. It says Muhammad was ordered. But the passage doesn't say who ordered him. So who ordered him?"

"Who are you to ask who ordered him?"

"I—"

"Are you trying to disprove the Hadith?"

He had a wooden pointer in his hand. "Come up here."

I went to the front of the room.

"Show me your palm."

I put out my hand.

He slashed the pointer across my palm.

"Ouch!"

"Good. Now leave your hand open."

He hit me nine more times. I couldn't hold back my tears. I had a giant welt across my hand.

"I hope this is a lesson to the rest of you," he said.

I was hauled before the headmaster again.

"So you have misbehaved again," he said, tapping the top of his walking stick.

"I asked a question. How am I supposed to convert others to Islam if I can't answer these questions?"

He turned his head from side to side and shook his gold-covered finger at me. "Next time you won't be punished in the class. Next time I will call an assembly, and you will be an example for every student."

CHAPTER 8

NO GOING BACK

I had been enrolled at the institute for more than two years when a few of us escorted some first-year students to the airport. The first-year students were traveling home on holiday. We spent the rest of that day sightseeing in Damascus. We ended up staying out later than we should have. It was close to three in the morning by the time we returned to campus. Midnight had marked the start of Ramadan, and eating was not permitted from dawn to sunset. That meant eating was prohibited after the start of the 4:00 morning prayer. Technically, we could eat up to that point.

Starving, we hustled down to the basement of the cafeteria. I cooked a pot of rice and added some onions, carrots, peas, and sauce. Despite the darkness, we took the pot outside, sat under a tree, and hurriedly scooped the rice mixture from the pot into our mouths with pita bread. It was after 4:30, and our fellow students were rising to prepare for morning prayer. A Turkish student looked down from the dorm window and spotted us.

Minutes later, Yusuf showed up. "What are you doing here?" he demanded.

Each of us had red sauce on our lips and pita in our hands.

"Infidels! Infidels! You are eating in violation of Ramadan."

He searched the ground for a stick. Finding none, he picked up a handful of sand, threw it down, and stormed off. Scared, we ran toward the cafeteria to dump the pot. Before we reached the door, we heard the giant bell ringing in the center of campus. That meant all students were to report to the assembly room at once.

We knew we were in trouble. My mates ran to the room at once. I stayed behind to put away our pot and clean up our mess. When I arrived at the assembly, Yusuf was ranting, and my friends were up front. They each had welts on their faces and tears in their eyes. Yusuf had beaten them in front of the student body.

All eyes were on me as I joined my friends at the head of the hall. I took my place at the end of the line, facing the student body. Yusuf approached.

"Infidel!" he shouted, spotting my face with his spit.

He slapped me across the face with such force that I stumbled and saw stars. When I regained my balance, he was so close to me that I could smell his rotten breath. I reared back and punched him in the face, landing a solid hit square on his nose. His lost his balance and his three-hundred-pound frame landed with a thud on the floor.

My friends froze. I'm not sure what shocked them more, the fact that Yusuf was on the ground with blood trickling from his nose, or that I had delivered the blow. I was probably the last person they'd expect to display violence. I didn't have an aggressive bone in my body, and I had never been in a fistfight. But something inside me had snapped.

Yusuf reached for his nose to see if it was broken. A sense of doom suddenly swept over me. I darted away, and the student body parted like the Red Sea. My four mates ran behind me.

"Stop!" Yusuf shouted.

We never looked back, sprinting through the courtyard, out the main gate of the institute, all the way to a transit bus a few blocks from campus. We jumped aboard just as the driver was about to pull away.

"You went too far," one of my friends said between breaths.

"I don't know what happened back there," I said, panting. "I just couldn't take that bully anymore."

"What are we going to do now?" one of them asked.

"I don't know."

We sat in silence as the bus made the thirty-minute journey to downtown Damascus. It dropped us off in Al-Marje Square. Stepping off the bus, I looked at the spot where Israeli spy Eli Cohen was hanged and wondered if I was headed to a similar fate.

"Where do we go from here?" one of the guys said.

"I don't know."

"No? You have to know. You caused this trouble for us."

I wanted to kick myself for eating after the start of Ramadan. It was a poor judgment. But I didn't think we deserved to be called infidels. In my mind, Yusuf was the wicked one. He fancied himself a religious leader. Yet he was nothing more than a tyrant who took pleasure in intimidating teenage boys. This time when he beat us I just had to act. The Qur'an tells Muslims to defend the weak and the helpless. I felt a duty to come to the aid of my friends.

But there was more to it than that. As far back as I could remember, violence had been the method for ensuring my obedience. My whole life I had been afraid to make a mistake out of fear that I would be beaten. I memorized the Qur'an at a remarkably young age, in part because I didn't want to face the wrath of my father. For the same reason I never missed prayers. To a certain extent I was tired of operating out of fear, particularly when it came to religion.

Islam, at least the way it was taught at the institute, was starting to feel more like devotion to rules than devotion to God. And the administration of harsh punishments was more important than any other aspects of the faith. Technically, I knew we were in violation of Islamic law by taking a few bites of food minutes after the start of a religious fast. But what about repentance and forgiveness? Those are big concepts in the Qur'an and core tenets of Islam. Yet the religious leaders were quick to deliver a tongue-lashing and a beating. The gravity of the offense and the severity of the punishment were out of balance.

After wandering the streets aimlessly for a number of hours, I knew we had to do something. We mulled over our options. They weren't good. The sun would soon be setting, and we had no place to sleep. We had no food and almost no money. Everything we owned—clothing, toiletries, and cash—was back at the institute. Plus, we were in a foreign country. We had no choice, it seemed, other than to return to the institute and face the consequences. Then I had an idea.

"Let's go to the police station," I said.

"What will we tell them?"

"What happened," I said. "We'll tell them what happened to us."

The others shrugged their shoulders and followed me.

I'd never been in a police station before. The one we entered in downtown Damascus had an officer stationed just inside the door.

"We have a complaint to make," I said.

Without saying a word, he pointed to a counter. Three officers were standing behind it. The one in the middle looked older than the other two, and he had a big mustache. My hands were shaking uncontrollably when I approached.

"What?" the man in the middle said.

"We have a complaint to make," I said. Then I started crying. I just lost control.

"Sit down," the officer said, directing us to some metal chairs along the wall.

He came out from around the counter and sat with us. "Relax," he said, putting up his hands, signaling us to stop and collect ourselves.

"We are students from El-Furquan Institute," I began, rubbing my eyes with my fists. I removed my cap. I couldn't stop crying.

"Relax," he said.

"We went to say good-bye to some of our colleagues at the airport. We got home really late at night. We forgot that Ramadan had started."

I put my hand over my mouth. "I'm sorry. Happy Ramadan."

"Unto you, too," the officer said.

"So we hadn't eaten all day. We went to the kitchen to cook. We were eating when one of the teachers found us. He started beating the hell out of us. So we ran away."

"He beat you?"

"Yes."

The officer looked at the others. "Did he beat you?"

They each nodded their head up and down.

"That school is always having problems," he said.

"We are afraid, sir," I said.

"Here's what you're going to do. You are going to go back to the school and pretend like nothing happened. And if that man ever beats you again, you come back here and tell me."

I felt better when we left. But my friends complained.

"I thought the police would give us an escort back to the school," one of them said.

"Yes. And have an officer go in and talk to school officials," another chimed in.

"Why didn't you say that to the officer?" I said. "Now you're out here complaining. You want to go back inside and talk to the police?"

"No."

"Then let's go back to the school. If anything happens, we'll come back here."

It was dark by the time we reached campus. Few lights were on, and the main gate was locked. Then we spotted one of our friends walking toward the building that housed many of the students. We motioned him toward us.

"Open the gate," I said.

"No."

"Why?"

"You don't know how much trouble you've caused here."

"What do you mean?"

"Read the notice board," he said. "Your names are on it. You've been expelled."

"What?"

"You've been expelled," he repeated. "You better go."

"Wait," I said. "Go get the assistant to the headmaster."

I knew him pretty well. He was one of the few reasonable guys at the institute. Several minutes later he appeared at the gate. For a moment he stood there shaking his head. He had thick, curly black hair and light skin. He was from Morocco. Finally, he opened the gate and led us to his office. We each took a seat.

"Yusuf was beating us," I said.

"Well, you beat him back. That was your big mistake."

He read from Hadith. "You have to respect a teacher. A teacher is more like a prophet." He looked up at me. "Can you beat a prophet?"

"Never."

"But you did. You beat a teacher."

I dropped my head.

"You have been expelled. All of you. You are leaving tomorrow."

A lump formed in my throat. The other guys looked at me. My two cousins were in the group. They, in particular, were furious with me. The three of us would have hell to pay when we got home. Under Islamic law we were going to have to be judged for what we had done. Non-Muslims have little understanding of how this works.

The sacred law of Islam is known as Sharia, which is interpreted as "the path to the watering place." The Qur'an, first and foremost, is the source of Islamic law. In all, the Qur'an contains seventy verses discussing personal laws, seventy verses on civil laws, thirty on penal laws, and twenty on judiciary matters. Derived from the Qur'an and the prophet Muhammad's life, Sharia pertains to all facets of law, from such civil matters as crime, politics, and economics to such personal matters as hygiene, sexuality, and diet. Islamic judges apply Sharia.

In my community in Nigeria, the imam had authorized Islamic judges to adjudicate personal, family, and community affairs under Sharia. These proceedings were called tribunals. They were typically one-sided affairs in which the elders served as judge and jury. Witnesses generally were not called, and the subject of a tribunal has no legal representative.

I wasn't looking forward to any of this. None of us were.

CHAPTER 9

LETTER OF THE LAW

My cousins and I arrived back at our village together. It was not a glorious homecoming. People shunned us. The village elders stayed away too. They were saving their wrath for the trial. My father glared at me in stony silence. He was one of the elders who would be judging me. I knew he'd be my harshest critic.

My mother was the only one happy to see me. At least she was the only one who showed it. She threw her arms around me and reminded me that she was the one telling everyone that I was too young to go away to Syria. She was right. But nobody listened to her.

When I felt the safety of her arms, I wanted to stay there. It was wishful thinking. The trial was scheduled for the following morning.

That night I couldn't sleep. On top of everything else, I found out that my cousins had turned against me. The minute we got home they went to the elders and reported that I was responsible for the entire episode in Damascus. Worse, they reported that I had stirred up a rebellion at the institute. That was a lie. Nonetheless, they succeeded in getting out of the trial by agreeing to testify against me. Meantime, they kindled my father's rage against me.

I had always known that my stepbrothers were not my friends. But now my cousins were getting in on the act. It wasn't until that time that I realized they would go as far as to slay me. There had been instances of teenage girls being stabbed to death or strangled by their fathers during tribunal proceedings under Islamic law. These were known as honor killings, performed to extinguish shame and embarrassment from a family. I was sure I was doomed.

At dawn I went to the mosque for prayer service. My father was there. He saw me. But he acted as if I weren't there, as if I weren't his son. I felt inescapably guilty and unworthy. Nothing depressed me more than the sense that I had not measured up in my father's eyes. I knew that I hadn't just disappointed him. I had humiliated him. I hated myself for that.

Immediately after prayers, my father left the mosque. I stayed behind to read the Qur'an and meditate. I stayed there until noon. Then someone summoned me to appear before the imam. The time had come for my tribunal to start.

When I exited the mosque, I found the imam seated on the ve-randah. Eight elders—including my father—flanked him in a semi-circle. All were wearing traditional gowns and caps, and all were staring at me with cold expressions. No one said a word.

I'd witnessed enough tribunals that I knew what to do. I took a seat on the porch floor, my legs crossed under me. Four teenagers—including two of the imam's sons—filed in around me to witness the proceeding.

"How are you?" the imam said. His voice was pleasant but firm.

"Thank God," I said in a very low voice. It was the best answer I could give under the circumstances.

"Welcome back," he said.

"Thank you," I whispered.

The moment the imam had completed his greeting, one of his senior elders started in on me. "So you think what you did was the right thing to do?"

It wasn't really a question. It was more of an accusation, and I was not given a chance to respond.

"How can you do this?" the elder continued. "You shock us. You disappoint us."

Again I said nothing.

"You disgrace us," another elder shouted.

It doesn't take long in these tribunals for the elders to start shouting over the top of each other in their race to levy accusations. There is no point in trying to rebut them. That only adds fuel to the fire.

Another elder accused me of violating Ramadan and chastised me for striking a teacher.

"You embarrass the imam," an elder shouted.

"You have disgraced your family and your father," another one chimed in. "Are you happy now?"

By that point I was trembling and crying. I buried my face in my hands. I wanted my father to come to my defense, but he was angrier than any of them. In a rage, he rose to his feet. His hands were shaking, and the veins were visible in his forehead and neck. "Let me kill him," he shouted.

I froze when my father lunged at me. One of the elders jumped up and tackled my father from behind. Others jumped in. I started backing up. Finally, the imam had seen enough.

"All right," he shouted. "All right."

My father stopped. So did everyone else.

"The boy recognizes his fault," the imam said. "And he's ready to make amends."

It was the first sign of mercy in the entire ordeal.

The imam instructed my father to sit down.

He complied.

Once the imam asserted his authority, no one else spoke. Fortunately for me, the imam had a reputation for fairness. He was also my mother's cousin. Looking back, I can't help thinking that the latter must have influenced his approach toward me.

I wiped the tears from my cheeks and faced the imam, who pronounced his sentence. I would spend a year in exile, teaching Islamic studies at a primary school in the city of Gashua. Then I would spend an additional year in an Islamic institute in Nigeria, taking courses in Islamic studies.

I was speechless. It was an uncharacteristically light sentence under the circumstances.

"You see what you have caused?" the imam said to me.

I nodded.

"All of this," the imam continued, motioning to his elders and my father, "is because of you."

I nodded again.

He instructed me to go home and prepare to head to Gashua. I had three days to get ready. It was pretty clear that he had already made some arrangements with the school.

The elders were dismissed, and the tribunal was over.

The next day my father left town on business. He didn't bother saying good-bye. By the time he returned home, I had left for Gashua to live with my uncle and begin teaching at an Islamic school.

CHAPTER 10

SLAUGHTER THE GOAT

My first semester of teaching went well. I did everything expected of me. I stayed out of trouble. And I spent every free moment studying the Qur'an or attending the mosque. Then I had an opportunity to go home for one week.

As soon as my mother saw me, she feared I hadn't been eating enough.

"Are they feeding you?" she asked.

"Yes. They give me food every evening."

"What about the morning?"

"In the morning I have tea and some chocolate and usually milk. Some mornings I cook myself some eggs."

"What?"

"I know how to cook."

"What do you mean?"

"When I was in Syria, I learned how to cook for myself."

"You *cook?*" she asked. "How can a man cook?"

"All of us boys at the institute in Damascus cooked. We had to."

"When a young man goes in the kitchen, he will never get a wife," she said, tears forming in her eyes. "Didn't I teach you that?"

That's the Hausa tradition. I didn't have the heart to tell her that Damascus wasn't the only place where the Hausa tradition is ignored. Muslim men in other parts of Nigeria were cooking too. Even in Gashua, men knew how to cook. Still, my mother preferred to blame the fact that I was cooking on the boarding school in Damascus.

"It is good that you ran away from that place," she whispered.

"It's all right," I told her, patting her on the shoulder and trying to assure her that I would one day find a wife.

But the situation wasn't all right in her mind. She couldn't accept it.

On the second day of my visit home I was relaxing under the neem tree across the street from our home when one of my ten-year-old nephews bounded out of the house. "Muhammad. Muhammad."

"What? What is it?" I asked him.

"Nobody is around to slaughter the goat," he said.

It was a Wednesday. Traditionally, my father would always slaughter a goat on Wednesdays and give it to my mother, who would gut it and clean it before cooking the meat. She could feed our entire family and some of our neighbors on one goat. The problem was that my father wasn't back from his business trip. Whenever he was gone, another man, such as one of my uncles, would slaughter the goat for him. But on this particular Wednesday, no other men were readily available, and my mother was waiting.

"You have to do it," my nephew said.

In all my years of being around this practice and watching my father and plenty of other men slaughter goats, I had never done it myself.

I told my nephew to go to the kitchen and retrieve my father's

fifteen-inch knife and meet me at the pen near the edge of our compound. The goat was already in a separate holding pen. I led him
out and pushed him down on the ground, where I tied his four legs
together with rope. In accordance with Islamic tradition, I made
sure his head was facing toward Mecca.

My nephew handed me the knife.

"Now hold his legs down," I told him.

The goat started bleating.

I put my left hand over its mouth. With my right hand I put the
knife to his throat, aligning the blade with the two main veins that
run along the neck.

"In the name of Allah," I said, as I slit the animal's throat. Blood
shot into the air, and the goat trembled, as if its spirit was leaving its
body. Blood streamed steadily into the parched, sandy ground.

Sick to my stomach, I held the animal down until it stopped
bleeding. It took about fifteen minutes. Then I stepped back.

It was my first slaughter, and I had performed it in accordance
with Islamic ritual. Yet I felt guilty, as if I had done something hor-
ribly wrong. The boys were looking at me. Silent, I turned and
walked away.

By that evening, my mother had boiled the goat meat to a soft,
tender state. She served it with rice and a spicy pumpkin sauce. It
was one of my favorite dishes. But that night all I could visualize
was blood. I pretended I didn't feel well and excused myself from
the meal.

After dinner I sneaked out of the compound and walked two
blocks to a nearby stand, where I purchased tea, milk, and bread
from the vendor. That was my dinner. It was all I ate for the rest of
my week at home.

My father didn't speak to me during my visit. His anger toward me had not cooled. Months passed before I spoke to him.
The silence, in many respects, was more cutting than his shouting

or his violence. Day after day, I woke up with guilt, shame, and embarrassment.

The whole experience drained my enthusiasm for the clergy. I had been incredibly faithful throughout all my boyhood and teenage years. I had done everything my father asked. And I'd missed out on a lot while being consumed with prayers, rituals, and scripture study. It was as if my one mistake in Damascus had negated nearly twenty years of obedience and diligence. That began to grate on me.

So did all the hypocrisy. My father was so rigidly focused on punishment that he completely overlooked the spirit of Islam's teachings. In some ways he was no different from the instructors at the institute in Damascus. I don't like admitting that. But it's how I felt at the time.

Needless to say, I was having a hard time picturing myself as a member of the clergy, especially in my home village. Yet I went off and fulfilled the requirements outlined by the imam, dedicating the next year to teaching and studying while in exile. While I was away, the imam and a number of his counselors persuaded my father that the best thing for me was to transfer to Cairo to complete my college education at Al-Azhar University.

At first, my father resisted for purely political reasons. He hated Egypt's president, Anwar Sadat, for engaging in peace talks with Israel, a nation that my father described as full of infidels. Sadat, he complained, had sold out and corrupted Egypt by reaching a peace pact with the Israelis.

But the imam prevailed on him, pointing out that Al-Azhar, a Muslim university in Cairo, would properly educate me in the virtues of Islam and the evils of the West. The first pleasant conversation I had with my father in more than a year occurred after he gave his blessing for me to attend Al-Azhar.

Just the fact that Al-Azhar had put us back on speaking terms made me want to enroll there. Despite all that had happened, I still longed to redeem myself in my father's eyes.

My mother also embraced the plan. As much as she preferred to keep me closer to home, she had come to believe that the best thing for me was to study in Cairo. If nothing else, it kept my father happy, which meant peace at home. But she also hoped that a degree in Islamic studies from Al-Azhar would rehabilitate my chances of becoming an imam in Nigeria.

I promised my mother that I would do my absolute best in Egypt. This time, I assured her, I would return with honor and with a degree. She liked that. My father did too.

CHAPTER 11

AL-AZHAR

Excited, I burst into our house with my brand-new passport and student visa in hand. It was October 6, 1981, and I was officially cleared to go to Egypt. Waving my travel documents above my head, I encountered my cousin in the living room.

"Look," I said.

"Hey, your president is dead," he announced. He had an evil grin.

"What are you talking about?" I asked.

"Anwar Sadat."

I turned up my hands. "What about him?"

"They just assassinated him this morning," my cousin boasted.

He took a lot of satisfaction in saying that. He was gloating. I felt sick. *Impossible*, I thought.

Over the next few days the news filtered through our village. Islamist nationalists in league with the Muslim Brotherhood had carried out the brazen attack. The two groups were angry over the 1978 Camp David accords and Sadat's willingness to sign a peace treaty with Israel in 1979. Islamic militants in the Egyptian army decided to strike during a parade that was intended to celebrate President Sadat's momentous achievements toward peace. Soldiers jumped out of an army truck and approached the reviewing stand, where President Sadat and his entourage were seated. One soldier threw a grenade while others opened fire on the president. A riot broke out as blood streamed from the area, and those who escaped the gunfire were trampled in their frantic attempts to escape the scene. Sadat was pronounced dead shortly after being rushed to a nearby military hospital.

I became instantly depressed. Unlike my father and many members of my family, I had admired and respected Sadat as a man of peace. I viewed his death as a huge loss to the Arab world.

I also couldn't help worrying that my plan to study in Egypt had been derailed. The airport in Cairo was shut down indefinitely. The country seemed in chaos. Even the peace accord with Israel was called into question. Everything was up in the air, including my future.

But Egypt's vice president, Hosni Mubarak, wasted no time trying to put those fears to rest. Immediately after assuming power, he addressed the nation and affirmed Egypt's commitment to all of its treaties and charters. He also put the country under martial law.

I left for Cairo on October 22, the day the airport there reopened. The moment I got off the plane in Egypt, I was patted down. Women were taken into private rooms and searched. Guards opened my bags and rifled through everything, including every shirt and pants pocket. They even went page by page through each book in my suitcase. The military presence in the airport surpassed what I had seen in Syria.

The first time I saw military men with guns, in Damascus, I was scared. I was sixteen then. Now, about to turn twenty-one, I welcomed the sight of men in uniform. They gave me a sense of security. I had changed a lot since passing through Cairo five years earlier.

Once I finally made it out of the airport, I observed that Cairo had changed a lot too. As a taxi took me through the city, I saw no food lines snaking down sidewalks and around buildings. Five years earlier people had been hungry. There were no piles of garbage, either. The overhead electrical cables for the public buses had vanished too. There was a brand-new, aboveground tram system. The streets were clean, and people were wearing newer, stylish clothing.

I attributed these improvements to Sadat's decision to enter into a peace treaty with Israel. But it was also clear that his assassination had cast a shadow over the city. That was particularly evident when I entered the section of the city where the presidential palace was. That area was known as "The City of the Sun." Jeeps were on every corner with military police, state security officials, and criminal investigators stopping vehicles and checking IDs. I chose to look for an apartment in that neighborhood because I figured it was the safest place in the city.

It didn't take me long to find a rental listing for a studio apartment inside a two-story home that was encircled by a concrete wall. It was on a residential street where lots of white children were tossing Frisbees and playing some game with a stick and a ball. The other odd thing was the presence of so many attractive blond girls wearing blue jeans and pushing baby strollers. For mothers, they were remarkably thin.

My landlady was an Egyptian Greek. Her name was Bethesda. She was a widow who lived upstairs and rented the downstairs of her home. Two Arab girls from Saudi Arabia had one apartment. I took the studio across the hall. There was a garden full of jasmine in the backyard. Its fragrance wafted through the windows of the house. I liked that.

Bethesda taught me a lot about the neighborhood. First, most of the residents were Americans and Europeans, many of whom worked for the United Nations or at the various embassies or aid organizations. The game with the stick and ball was called baseball. And none of those thin blondes were moms. They were nannies. I'd never heard of a nanny. Bethesda said nannies are rich girls hired by rich families to take care of rich babies.

The City of the Sun could not have been more different from my hometown. But I liked it. The streets were clean. The people were friendly. And I had easy access to good food. The first night I was there I ate chicken and rice at a local café. That's when I discovered that Cairo had the best lemonade I've ever tasted—sweet and loaded with sugar. I drank glass after glass.

After securing a place to live, I found a mosque. I chose one within walking distance. The minute I entered I knew I was in for a new experience. The place was enormous. Massive white columns with gold trim lined the hall, and thousands of men occupied prayer mats. I was so far back that I couldn't see the imam. But I could hear him through loudspeakers positioned throughout the mosque. He was speaking about Sadat's assassination and the current political climate in the Middle East.

I had never heard an imam talk politics during prayer time. I had never seen men cry in a mosque, either. But many men wept as the imam talked about Sadat and what his loss would mean to Egypt. "Allah will punish those men for their evil," he warned. "And bless those who do good."

"Praise be to Allah," the men repeated. When thousands of men said those words in unison, the hair stood up on my arms. I felt like I was in Allah's army. The best part was that no one was advocating violence. That was refreshing.

My apartment was quite a distance from campus. Founded in 988, Al-Azhar University is generally regarded as the oldest Islamic university in the world. Only Muslims are admitted. The promotion of Islamic religion and culture is part of the school's mission.

The faculty is composed of the finest scholars in the Muslim world. Known for excellence in logic, grammar, and rhetoric, the school produces some of the world's leading authorities on medicine and engineering. The university's library rivals the Egyptian National Library and Archives.

The university is closely associated with Al-Azhar Mosque, built by Jawhar the Sicilian roughly seventeen years before the university opened. Historians believe that the mosque was named after the prophet Muhammad's daughter Fatima al-Zahraa. It is the most famous mosque in the Muslim world.

The university and the mosque create a powerful fusion between academia and religion. A supreme council governs the school, and Sheikh Al-Azhar, a grand imam, heads the council. Until the 1950s, Al-Azhar issued fatwas. These religious edicts carried great weight in the Muslim world. When I arrived on campus in the fall of 1981, Al-Azhar still maintained its supremacy as the center for Sunni Islamic thought in the Arab world. The sheer size of the campus was daunting. But it seemed like the perfect environment to resume the drive to become a cleric. That thought had reclaimed center stage in my mind. The fact that I had been granted a second chance gave rise to a renewed sense of purpose. This time, I told myself, I wasn't going to let my parents down. I planned on being a member of the clergy by the time I graduated.

Classes were not as rigorous as I expected. But the fervor over Islam was intense. Because I was pursuing a degree in Islamic studies, I took classes with some of the most extreme Muslims on campus. My peers were the future clerics of the Muslim world. Their rhetoric against the West was pronounced. Some of the professors in my major were militant in their views toward the West too. A couple of my professors even spoke openly against Israel in their lectures, always taking the side of the Palestinians. They held the view that Israel had taken the Holy Land by force and that the only way to get it back was by jihad.

AL-AZHAR

It didn't take me long to realize that Cairo was a diverse place. Even within Islam it was diverse. The tenor in the local mosque was favorable toward peace with Israel. The tenor on campus was the opposite. I disagreed with much of what I heard on campus. But after all that I had been through, I wasn't about to say anything to contradict the popular voice in my classes.

CHAPTER 12

WHAT IS LOVE?

For the first month of school, my life was confined to three things: attending class, attending mosque, and studying in my apartment. I didn't go anywhere else. The first time I left campus was to visit the Nigerian embassy to pick up a copy of my resident permit. With a map and some basic directions, I boarded a metro bus near my apartment.

The minute I sat down I made eye contact with a girl sitting opposite me. She had alluring bronze skin, honey-colored eyes, and shiny black hair braided like a crown on her head. I couldn't help glancing down at her high heels. Back home, high heels were associated with immoral women. But I sensed this girl was not one of those girls. The rest of her attire was in strict accordance with Sharia law. Her skirt went well below her knees, and she had on a shirt that had its collar folded over the round neck of her red sweater.

Still, I couldn't turn my eyes from her lower legs. Their slender shape and her rich tan stirred me. She was the most striking Arab woman I had ever laid eyes on.

Eventually, our eyes met, and she flashed a polite smile. I nodded and smiled back.

"Hello," she said politely in English.

"Hello. What is your name?"

"My name is L'amour."

"That's a pretty name."

"In French it means 'love.'"

"Wow!"

"But I go by Aaban."

"Aaban?"

"Yes. Now what is your name?"

"Muhammad."

"And where are you from, Muhammad?"

"Nigeria."

"Ah, the best people."

"And you?"

"I'm Sudanese. But I was born here in Cairo."

I wasn't used to talking with girls and didn't know what else to say. Luckily, she carried the conversation from there. She explained that her father was a diplomat for the Arab League and worked at the headquarters in Cairo. I told her I was a student at Al-Azhar. She said she was very familiar with the institution.

Her confidence made me nervous. She was so self-assured. And her beauty was overwhelming. I didn't quite know how to act. I had no experience with meeting women. As a teenager I'd been forbidden to have relationships with girls. So here I was, twenty years old, and I had never been on a date. From the time I was twelve I was always in such controlled environments as boarding schools and institutes that I simply had had no interaction with girls or women my age.

Yet I felt an instant attraction toward Aaban. It was a brand-new sensation. The feeling was so foreign that I was uneasy. I was unsure.

Is this love? I knew so little about that subject. Up to that time, my experience with love was limited to a couple of Shakespeare plays that I had read during boarding school in Nigeria: *Romeo & Juliet* and *As You Like It*.

Aaban and I made small talk until reaching El Tahrir Square, where I had to change buses. Aaban stood up, too. She could tell I looked a little lost, and she asked where I was headed. When I said the Nigerian embassy, she said she was heading in that direction and offered to show me the way.

We boarded another metro bus that took us to the Nile River, where we caught a water taxi. It was clear that Aaban had been on the river many times and knew her way around. I had only read about the Nile in books and brochures. The views from the boat took my breath away. I couldn't get over the riverside skyscrapers, the waterfront restaurants, and the mix of boats and bridges criss-crossing the water.

Aaban was like a tour guide, pointing out important landmarks and explaining everything we were seeing.

When we exited the boat, I was disappointed. I knew we were going to part ways, and I didn't want to. We'd been together less than thirty minutes. It was the best half hour since I had arrived in Egypt. She pointed me in the direction of the embassy, smiled, and said good-bye.

"Can I see you again?" I called out to her. I could hardly believe that I had the nerve to ask.

She stopped, looked over her shoulder, and gave me a funny look. "No."

Then she kept walking. I felt like an idiot.

After taking a few more steps, she stopped again and turned

toward me. "But we will surely meet by chance one day . . . just like today."

I had no idea what that meant. But I was sure I'd never see her again.

I took care of my business at the embassy and began the trek back to my apartment, trying to forget the beautiful woman I had just met. But I couldn't get her out of my mind. When I closed my eyes that night I saw her face. She was all I could think about. It was driving me mad. My emotions were all over the place. Even praying at the mosque was difficult—I couldn't get my mind off the girl. This went on for days.

I was feeling something else for the first time—longing. I was longing for Aaban. I was either in love or losing my mind. It also occurred to me that I might be sinning. The emotions inside me were so strong that I feared they might be improper. But maybe it was just the fact that they were new and therefore foreign.

Either way, I was anxious. I wanted to talk to someone about my situation. But I was afraid. My colleagues at Al-Azhar would surely look down on me for being so infatuated with a woman I barely knew. Even I was second-guessing myself.

This went on for about a week. Then one afternoon I stepped out of my apartment and saw a young woman with beautifully braided hair. I could only see her from behind. But my heart skipped a beat. I followed her up the street. Eventually she turned around. It was Aaban. She recognized me right away. I was stunned.

"Hey," she said, "what are you doing here?"

She extended her hand and looked pleased to see me.

"I live here," I told her, pointing to my street. "What are *you* doing here?"

She pointed up the street in the direction of a woman's college that was part of Ain Shams University. "That's where I attend school," she said.

"You are a *student?*"

She laughed. "Of course."

"I had no idea."

"I just finished classes for the day."

"What are you studying?"

"Psychology."

I nodded, unsure what to say next.

"Did you get your student visa straightened out?" she asked.

I nodded.

"Well, that's good."

I could feel myself sweating. I had a lump in my throat, and my heart was racing. "Can we sit somewhere and chat?" I blurted out.

"Sure," Aaban said.

Her answer caught me flatfooted. I guess I expected her to say no again. When she said yes, I didn't know where to go. She smiled and recommended a fast food place across the street.

We ordered hamburgers and started talking. The conversation centered on our families and our studies. Like me, she came from a strong, traditional Muslim family. We were also very similar in our seriousness toward education.

An hour went by in a flash. She had to catch a bus to another appointment. But this time when we parted, she accepted my invitation to meet again. We also exchanged phone numbers.

Over the next few weeks we saw each other almost daily. Our time together was spent entirely in conversation. We talked for hours about books, Arab and African traditions and cultures, arts, cinema, and literature. Aaban knew much more about movies because I had never been allowed to watch them. We were both well read and had a mutual affection for Shakespeare. She was in awe of my mastery of the Qur'an, and she admired my determination to become a religious leader. My seriousness about Islam fit neatly into her family's convictions.

For the remainder of the school year we were virtually inseparable when we weren't in class. Then one night Aaban took me to meet her older sister. That night we watched an Egyptian film. It was a love story. When the film ended, we found ourselves alone in Aaban's sister's apartment. As the film credits ended and the screen went black, we were side by side in the dark. Without thinking, I kissed her.

It was the first time I had ever kissed a girl. It felt electric, as if I had touched something forbidden and received a shock. I quickly came to my senses, pulling away. "I'm sorry."

She said nothing.

"I'm sorry," I repeated. "I didn't mean it."

Still silent, she nodded.

I walked home in shame that night.

After that incident, Aaban stopped taking my calls. When I tried dropping by her apartment, her roommate would say Aaban wasn't around. I knew that wasn't true. I had ruined everything with a kiss. Unbelievable!

The realization that I had scared Aaban away made it impossible for me to focus on my studies. I couldn't focus on anything. I became more and more irritable toward everyone around me. A week of no contact with Aaban felt like months. Then she showed up unannounced at my apartment. I opened the door, and we threw our arms around each other.

"I'm really sorry," I told her. "I didn't mean to go that far."

She looked at me with that familiar expression of disappointment. "You are foolish," she said.

"What do you mean?"

She brought her lips to mine. Suddenly I felt her tongue.

"What are you doing?" I shouted, pushing her away.

She laughed. "You *are* a foolish guy."

"I am apologizing, and you are going *further?*"

"If you really love me, how can you kiss me and say you're sorry for kissing me? It means you don't love me."

"Where I come from, you don't do that to your own wife."

She kissed me again. And again I felt her tongue.

"I feel like I am assaulting you by doing this," I told her.

She laughed. "Is that your African mentality?"

"In Nigeria we don't kiss. It's not in our culture. If you kiss your wife, she will call a family meeting, and there is big trouble."

"Oh, c'mon."

"There was a man in our village who kissed his wife while having sex with her. She sneaked out early the next morning, ran away to her family, and reported him. That day the man was confronted by her entire family."

"Are you telling me husbands don't even kiss their wives?"

"Yes."

"That is weird. Africans are backward."

"Are you not African? After all, you are from Sudan."

"I was born here, and I never had anything to do with Sudan. I only go there on holiday. Things in Sudan are backward too."

I took a deep breath. "I don't mind kissing on the cheek or even on the lips. But putting your tongue in my mouth is going too far. Where I come from, you can be called a witch for that."

"It's called a French kiss."

"French?"

"You've never heard of this?"

"No."

She gave me a funny look and put up her hands.

"In northern Nigeria, having sex is one thing. Kissing is another. Sex is a formality, not to be enjoyed. Romance, on the other hand, is lust. The devil is behind that."

"The devil is behind romance?"

"Yes. That's why a man can have multiple wives. The wives are like properties."

"There is no romantic love there?"

"It's not about that. The husband doesn't kiss his wives. He just has sex with them and has children. If he kisses them, that is lust. And lust is of the devil."

She laughed. "Your African mentality is so backward. You need to listen to some Arabic music, some love songs."

She put on a Umm Kulthum record and flirted with me, playfully pretending to seduce me. Suddenly there was a knock at the door. It was one of her girlfriends. Aaban let her in and immediately resumed flirting. Her friend put her hand on the back of my head and started pushing me closer to Aaban's lips. "She wants to kiss you," the girl said.

I pulled away.

"A million men would love to kiss Aaban," the girl said. "Yet you are pulling away."

"I will not do that in front of you," I said.

"All right," the girl said, coming toward me. "Then *I* will kiss *you*."

"No, no, no," I said, backing up.

"Well," she said, stopping, "I will leave you two alone."

She left, and the smile left Aaban's face. I had to do something. Without saying a word, I put my hands on her shoulders and French kissed her. I didn't want to. But I felt I had to. The moment I did, she started licking my tongue. It felt so prohibited. *I'm not supposed to even think of something like this, let alone do it,* I thought.

The longer we stood there, the more I liked kissing her.

CHAPTER 13

A NEW LENS

Cairo is a great tourist city. People come from all over the world to see the Great Pyramid of Giza, the Sphinx, and the Temples of Karnak. And every tourist has a camera. I decided I wanted one. In addition to photographing famous sites, I figured I'd take pictures of things I wanted to paint or draw.

The thought of purchasing a camera made me a little nervous. No one in my family owned a camera. My father had forbidden photography. Cameras, he felt, were a tool of the devil. But being around millions of people with cameras changed my view.

One weekend I went with a friend to Port Said. It was my first time to visit this city near the Suez Canal. We arrived mid-morning and found the streets bustling with people. We passed a storefront that had cameras in the window. I spotted a Minolta. The shop-keeper saw me pointing at it through the window. "Can I help you?"

"I want to buy a camera."

"Which one?"

"The Minolta."

He handed me the camera. "And this," he said, handing me a role of Fuji film, "is a gift." He showed me how to load the film. "Remember, never open the camera until you are sure the film is rolled back completely."

I nodded.

"Otherwise, the film will be exposed and all the pictures will be ruined."

Then he showed me the settings. "This one is for sunlight. This one is for evening."

I looked through the lens.

"And you can zoom in," he said, showing me how.

"Wow."

"This is the flash." He connected it to the top of the camera.

"I see."

He removed a black leather case from a box and draped it on my shoulder. Then he took the camera from my hands and placed it inside. "Now you are ready."

"Thank you," I said.

He grinned. "Time to pay."

I gave him 300 Egyptian pounds. "I can't wait to photograph something," I said to my friend.

"Whatever you do," the shopkeeper told me, "don't take pictures on the highway from here to Cairo. It is a military zone, and taking pictures is not allowed. They will seize your camera and arrest you."

"Thank you."

"Now, when you leave here, just wear your camera around your neck like a tourist. That way when you reach the border, they won't bother you."

Once I had the camera, the main thing I wanted to photograph was Aaban. One afternoon we were having lunch at a restaurant along the Nile. Her hair was braided, and two of the braids wrapped around the back of her head. She had on a khaki sweater over a white-collared shirt and a knee-length skirt. She looked amazing, sitting there sipping lemonade through a straw.

"I want to take your picture," I told her.

She just looked at me and smiled.

"I'm going home for the summer soon, and I want your picture."

"Are you afraid you won't remember me if you don't have a picture?"

I folded my arms across my chest.

"All right," she said.

We walked into the garden alongside the cafe. It was loaded with flowers.

"Stand here," I said, positioning her next to a tall flower. Then I looked through the lens, focusing on her face. Her olive-toned skin was silky smooth, and the mascara on her long black lashes really set off her honey-colored eyes. "You are the most beautiful piece of art a man can see. Smile."

She did. I clicked and clicked and clicked. Within minutes I had gone through almost an entire roll. I was down to my last picture when I spotted our waiter. "Will you take a picture of us?"

He obliged and then handed the camera back to me. "Baksheesh," he said.

I handed him some money.

"When you develop those pictures," Aaban said, "don't show them around. I haven't introduced you to my family yet. And I don't want them seeing those pictures before they meet you."

When I wasn't with Aaban, I hung out with a small group of students from the university. Most of them were Egyptians. All were Muslims. One afternoon we went out for lunch. Afterward, we were aimlessly wandering the streets when we came upon a theater. All the other guys in the group had seen plenty of movies. I was the only one who hadn't. When they decided to take in a matinee, I was uncomfortable but decided to go along.

The film was *Xanadu*, starring Olivia Newton John. I had never heard of her or the movie. After presenting our IDs to security, we filed into a row of seats toward the rear of the theater. I was surprised to see so many women in the audience. Women weren't allowed inside the theater in my hometown in Nigeria.

The minute Olivia Newton John appeared on screen with her blonde hair feathered back, I was captivated. Arab women simply didn't look like that. The men in the theater started whistling. There was so much noise that it was nearly impossible to make out the words being spoken on the screen. That hardly mattered, though. Everyone was caught up in the dancing and in Newton John's looks.

By the time she sang "Magic," the audience had turned raucous.

"She's a bitch!" the men around us shouted.

"Whore. Whore," other men yelled.

I wasn't accustomed to hearing that kind of language. But it was clear from the expressions and body language of those using these terms that they admired Olivia Newton John. They loved seeing a woman—especially a blonde one from the West—dance and strut like that. It was precisely the kind of thing that my father warned against when it came to the cinema.

I never told Aaban that I saw *Xanadu*. She would not have approved. I didn't approve, either. The whole scene was one I wanted to forget. Aaban helped me to see women in a different light. She was beautiful but dignified. It was actually a little intimidating to be around her at times. She had a take-charge approach, and she wasn't afraid to speak her mind. When it came to our courtship, she took the lead. Once she made up her mind that she wanted to marry me, she moved quickly and informed her parents. She didn't ask them. She told them.

I found that shocking. I just couldn't get over it. Women would never behave that way in Nigeria.

But that's where Aaban would say women shouldn't have to behave. They should just be.

It took me some time to come around to her way of thinking. But I got there. I just had to unlearn everything I knew.

Aaban's parents immediately approved of our courtship. As practicing Muslims, they particularly liked the fact that I was on track to obtain a degree in Islamic studies and join the clergy. That meant stability and prestige as well as security for Aaban.

But my parents weren't like her parents. They would not go along so easily. So I held off telling them about the engagement. I didn't even tell them about Aaban. That was going to be a difficult conversation. For one thing, I didn't know how to bring up the fact that I was seeing a girl. The subject was taboo, and I avoided it for as long as possible.

But my siblings were starting to rib me for not marrying. My brothers had taken wives, and my sisters had been taken as wives in their teen years. When I returned home on holiday at the end of my first year of school in Cairo, my sister Amina and I got into an argument about the fact that I was still single.

"By the time you leave home to go back to school, you will leave with your wife in hand," she said.

"There is no one here I want to marry," I told her.

It angered me that Amina was being confrontational. I had gone away with her for three weeks when she was married at fourteen. I cared for her. I sympathized with her. We were friends. All I could think was that she was jealous of me because I had been given the opportunity to go off to college and see the world. I had a lot more freedom than she had. But I didn't deserve her vengeance.

As we bickered, I unpacked my bag. A picture fell from inside one of my books. It was a portrait of Aaban that she had given me just before I flew home. In the portrait she had a gold chain around her neck. She looked like a Sudanese queen.

Amina picked up the five-by-seven photograph and inspected it. Then she flipped it over. Aaban had written the words: "To Muhammad with all my love."

"Mother!" Amina shouted. "Come. Come see your son."

My mother appeared in my room. "What?"

"This," Amina said, handing her the photograph.

"It is a postcard?"

"Look on the back," Amina said.

Mother flipped it over and read the words from Aaban. "Somebody sent you a postcard. But there's no stamp on the back."

"It's not a postcard," Amina told her. "Aaban is the name of a girl."

My mother looked at the picture again. Then she looked at my sister. "You mean a girl sent this to him?"

"Yes. You people sit here and think he's down there in Cairo studying. But this is what he's doing."

My mother turned to me. "Is what your sister is saying true?"

"Aaban is my friend. She loves me."

Mother looked at Aaban's face again. Then a smile swept across her face. "*She* is really *your* friend?"

"Yes."

"She is an Arab girl?"

"Yes. She is a student at the university near my apartment."

"She is beautiful!"

I smiled. "Yes."

"And you deserve her."

"Thank you."

Amina snatched the picture from my mother's hand. "When Daddy comes home, I will show him."

I had a few more days before my father returned from a business trip. As soon as he got home, my sister Amina cornered him. A few minutes later my younger sister appeared in my bedroom.

"Daddy wants to see you."

"Why?"

"You are in trouble."

"Why am I in trouble?"

"Amina discovered your pictures."

"What?"

I pulled from beneath my bed the duffel bag where I had stashed all the photographs I had taken of Aaban, along with many of my other pictures of Egypt. The pictures were gone.

"I'm not the one who showed Amina where they were," my younger sister said.

When I entered the sitting room, my mother and Amina flanked my father. He was holding my photographs. "Explain this to me," he said.

I said nothing.

"I send you to school, and this is what you are doing again?"

I kept quiet.

"So you can never change. I have beaten you. And still you do this. You can't change. First you were drawing. Now you are taking pictures."

"He's a child," my mother said.

"He's no more a child," my father shouted. "He's in the university. He should be married and have children, like his age mates. His age mates already have two or three children."

"But he's still a student, and he is still studying."

"Nonsense, woman! Most of his age mates are students too. But they are married."

"This time when you leave home to go back to school," Amina interjected, "you will leave with your wife in your hand. We're going to make sure."

"He's not going back to school," my father fumed. "He's not going anywhere again."

"Abdul?" my mother said meekly. "What is this you are saying?"

"Cairo is bad news! From the beginning I said this. But the imam insisted. And this is why I don't like Egypt. It is a corrupt nation. Sadat is gone, and Mubarak is worse than he was."

"God is great," boomed the voice of the imam's assistant

116

through the compound loudspeaker. "I testify that Allah is the only God and Muhammad is his prophet. Come along to pray."

It was prayer time. My father turned to my mother. "Get r-r-rid of these pictures," he shouted, throwing my pictures on the floor. "Burn them!"

He stormed off to the mosque while my mother gathered up my photographs. They wouldn't exist by the time I returned from the midday prayer. Mother had no choice but to obey my father. My emotions were a mess of anger, betrayal, and sadness. I couldn't believe that my sister had stabbed me in the back, especially after all I had done to comfort her when she was forced to marry at fourteen and was sent off to a strange city. And I didn't know how I would last all summer without pictures of Aaban. I trudged off to the mosque and found a place in the back, as far away from my father as possible.

The only good news was that my father didn't know about my camera. Fortunately, I hadn't stored it under my bed with my pictures. I kept it well hidden and didn't tell anyone in my family about it. In fact, I didn't talk to my family about anything after they destroyed my pictures. I was pretty much a hermit for the next few weeks, until my father left on another of his business trips. That's when my mother came to my room and handed me an envelope. "Your pictures are here," she whispered. "Everybody thinks I got rid of them. Hide them. Don't leave them around here."

I threw my arms around her. It was as if she had given Aaban back to me.

"Who is Aaban?" she asked.

"She was born in Egypt. Her father works with the Arab League."

"The Arab League. That is a good thing."

"Yes. And she cooks for me and helps me clean."

"Very good."

"I want to marry her. Her parents want me to marry her. But I can't talk to you about it. I'm afraid of the kind of problems we had with the pictures."

"You know better than to bring pictures into this house."

"It won't happen again."

"Next time you come home, your sister won't be here. That would be a good time to discuss Aaban."

"What about father?"

"He will be better then."

She turned to leave.

"Mother?"

"What?"

"I want to take your picture."

"What?"

"I want to take your picture."

"You want to include me in your troubles?"

"No. I don't have a picture of you. I want one."

"You know I can't do that."

"I won't get the film developed here. I'll take it back to Cairo."

She stood silent for a moment. She was nearly fifty years old and had never been photographed. She'd never seen her face in a picture.

Suddenly a grin crept across her face. "I have to go change my headscarf."

I couldn't believe she was going to do it. I dashed outside to get my camera. My mother met me behind the house. I hung one of her wraps on the concrete wall for a backdrop.

"Stand in front of it," I told her.

She didn't know what to do.

"Look at the camera," I said.

Looking through the lens, I could see her fear. She was jittery and had creases on her forehead. She kept looking over my shoulder to make sure no one could see us.

"Try to relax."

She had on a coral necklace and big gold earrings, with a multi-colored headscarf that matched her wrap. Her hair and almost all of her body was covered. Only her face was visible. Her dark, deepset eyes reminded me of Aaban's.

"Smile," I said.

As soon as she did, I clicked.

"You are a beautiful woman."

She blushed. "We are finished now."

"Wait. It's better to take more than one in case the picture isn't clear. Let's take a couple more."

"Do it quickly."

Six months passed before I was able to show my mother her pictures. I took them home on a holiday visit and waited for a day when my father wasn't home.

"I developed the pictures. Can I show you?"

"No."

"But I want you to see them."

"You brought them here?"

"Yes."

"You told me you'd leave them in Cairo."

"I just want you to see them, and I'll take them back."

"That was not our agreement."

"Just two minutes. Then you can burn them if you want. I have the negatives back in Cairo and can print more."

She grew quiet. I removed the pictures from my satchel. She was speechless when she saw herself. Her eyes widened and then filled with tears. I think it was one of the happiest moments of her life. But it really was only a moment.

"You say you can print another copy of these?"

"Yes."

She walked outside and threw the photographs in the fire.

I heard her weeping as she did it. But she was grateful to me for the moment. It's remarkable to think that in my mother's entire life she felt like a pretty woman only once.

CHAPTER 14

TRANSFORMATION

My courtship with Aaban continued through our first two years of college. During that time I achieved high grades and maintained a steady dedication to the rituals and traditions of Islam. The combination of being enrolled in college and preparing for marriage sharpened my focus and restored my determination to be an imam. Eventually my father recognized that and became convinced that Aaban was good for me. Once he accepted Aaban, he started attending prayers at the mosque with me when I was home on holiday visits. He could see that I displayed all the outward signs of devotion. My prayers, my attire, and my mastery of the Qur'an made him proud. He was so pleased, in fact, that he gave his blessing for me to marry Aaban.

My relationship with my father hadn't been that good since I left home at sixteen to attend the institute in Damascus. For the first time since then I felt like everything was clicking—university studies, religious performance, and my relationship with Aaban. I felt on top of the world.

In December of 1983 I accepted a friend's invitation to attend a Christmas Eve party in Cairo. I didn't celebrate Christmas, but it was a big deal in Egypt. Jesus had been brought there by Mary and Joseph to escape the wrath of Herod the Great. Tradition holds that the apostle Mark subsequently established Christianity in Alexandria around A.D. 42, giving rise to Egyptian Coptic Christianity, which eventually spread throughout the country. Although orthodox Egyptian Christians still use the Coptic calendar and therefore celebrate the birth of Jesus on January 7, many Westerners flock to Egypt to celebrate the holiday on December 25. By mid-December, homes and churches throughout Cairo are decorated with lights, trees, candles, and mangers.

When my Muslim friend Abraham said he was going with other students to an off-campus Christmas celebration, I pictured an atmosphere with festive music and the customary Egyptian holiday foods. Partly out of curiosity, I decided to tag along.

The plan was to meet at Abraham's apartment and go from there. When I arrived, Abraham invited me inside while he finished getting ready. He led me to his bedroom, saying he had something to show me. The moment we entered the room, I spotted a bunch of Western shirts spread out on the bed—orange ones, yellow ones, and blue ones. "They're from Paris," Abraham bragged.

To me the colors were loud and the style was immodest; the shirts were certainly not the kind of clothing a Muslim should wear. Abraham, however, had had a different upbringing. He was from Mali, a West African country that gained its independence from France in 1960. His family relocated to Cairo when Abraham entered college. His family practiced Islam, but they weren't nearly as orthodox as Muslims from Nigeria. On his frequent visits to Paris, Abraham usually returned with things he purchased there.

He displayed something else he had recently bought—a record

album. He put it on his record player and dropped the needle. The beat and the lyrics seized me.

I didn't know what I was hearing.

Abraham told me it was "Hotel California" by The Eagles.

That didn't mean anything to me. But I was certain that the music was from hell. For my entire life I had dutifully avoided exposure to evil noises. My father had taught me that almost all music is evil and should be shunned. I had been trained to cover my ears whenever I was around music. Aaban didn't listen to Western music, either.

Abraham didn't see the harm. Then his sister Fatu entered the room. She was a couple years younger than I, and she closely resembled the Jamaican-American singer Grace Jones. She went out of her way to look like Jones, too. She kept her hair razor short on the sides and cropped at the top. She wore bright red lipstick.

She removed The Eagles record and put a different one on the record player. "Have you heard the latest album by Michael Jackson?" she asked me.

I gave her a puzzled look. "Who is Mike Jackson?"

She laughed at me.

Jackson's *Thriller* album had been released in the United States toward the end of 1982 and quickly emerged as one of the most popular records in the world. A year after the record's release, it was still producing Top 40 singles. Songs like "Beat It," "Billie Jean," "Human Nature," and "Wanna Be Startin' Somethin'" had become immensely popular in the club scene in Cairo.

But I didn't know any of that. I had never been to a club.

Fatu told her brother to play the Michael Jackson record for me.

The fast tempo and disco beat of "Wanna Be Startin' Somethin'" was unlike anything I had ever heard. Horns accentuated percussion. Then came that voice.

I assumed Jackson was a woman.

Fatu handed me the album cover. I was surprised to see that

Jackson was a man. Fatu began gyrating to the beat, moving her hips provocatively as her feet glided across the floor.

"Yeah, yeah," she sang along.

Her body looked amazing, especially her eyes and lips. Shell-shocked, I took a few steps back.

"Dance with me," she said, grinning and motioning me toward her with her index finger.

I shook my head and took a few more steps back. By now her body was moving in sync with the music.

Abraham took his sister's hand, and the two of them started dancing. As they laughed and carried on, I could hardly bear to watch. I just couldn't believe what I was seeing. Eventually, the commotion drew their mother to the bedroom. I was sure the carrying on would finally stop.

It didn't. Their mother smiled at Fatu, who was attempting to moon walk across the bedroom floor.

"Won't you join them?" their mother asked me.

I put up my hands and told her no.

These people are behaving like unbelievers, I thought. The immoral music and lewd dancing was an affront to the traditions and values of Islam. Yet Abraham, Fatu, and their mother were Muslims.

When the song ended, Abraham and Fatu told their mother they were heading to a party. I was sure I must have heard Abraham wrong. Fatu couldn't possibly be going with us. Where I came from, Muslims never permitted a girl to go out to a party at night. That tradition was precisely why I hadn't brought Aaban along that night.

I turned to Fatu's mother, fully expecting her to tell Fatu that she must stay home.

"Have a good time," she said.

I shook my head in disbelief as I followed my friends out the door and down the street. We passed by a pub. Through the window

Abraham spotted some friends and insisted on ducking inside to say hello. He promised me that we'd only be a minute.

My heart started racing the moment we entered the place. The music was so loud that people had to yell to be heard. The smell of alcohol permeated the air. One of the guys offered me a drink. Another guy offered me a smoke. I waved them both off. I feared that someone who knew me would walk past the pub window and spot me in this wicked environment. The chances were slim, but still my conscience was telling me to get out of there right away.

Abraham sensed my discomfort. He bade his friends farewell and hurriedly led me back outside. Relieved, I took a deep breath. A few minutes later we reached the party, which was held in a high-rise overlooking the Nile River. When I exited the elevator on the seventh floor, I saw a giant Christmas tree decorated with colorful ornaments and balloons. But the music blaring from the hall wasn't holiday music. I recognized the voice instantly: Michael Jackson.

Fatu knew every word to "Thriller" and started lip-syncing before we were even inside. I had a bad feeling, like I should leave. But I didn't.

Then a tall, handsome African man extended a hand and invited us toward the dance floor and cash bar. I immediately recognized the man as a student from Al-Azhar. I couldn't imagine what he was doing in this kind of environment.

As I stepped inside the dance hall, I spotted lots of European women wearing short skirts and tight blouses. They were all dancing wildly to "Thriller." Their bodies pulsing to every beat, these women looked terribly seductive. Most of the men dancing with these women were Muslims. I knew because I recognized some of them from Al-Azhar. Yet, here they were with a drink in one hand while carrying on with Western women. It was not what I expected to encounter.

A host offered me a drink. I had never tasted alcohol in my life. I said I'd take a Coke.

Meantime, I couldn't stop staring at the women. To be honest, I was gawking. Their movements and their attire were far more provocative than anything Olivia Newton John had done or worn in *Xanadu*, that's for sure. I had never seen women behave this way. Aaban certainly never dressed or moved that way. My mind was wandering into strange territory. God, I feared, would surely punish me for my thoughts and for being in such an evil environment.

When the DJ put on "Billie Jean," everyone at the party flocked to the floor. The frenzied atmosphere drove me to the balcony. Alone, I sank into a chair and stared down on the Nile, my mind a wreck of confusion. Muslim men cavorting with scantily dressed women. Bodies coming together. Alcohol flowing. Music blaring. It was the kind of environment that provoked God's rage. At least that's what I had been taught to believe.

Afraid to go back inside, I remained on the balcony. After what seemed like an hour or more, it finally dawned on me that the volume and tempo of the music had changed. A soft ballad had started. Before I knew it, Fatu was at my side, pulling me toward the dance floor. When she took my hand and flashed her sultry smile, I could smell the rich scent of her French perfume. My power to resist evaporated like morning dew under the rising the sun.

On the dance floor she took my hands and placed them on her hips. Then she wrapped her arms around my neck. Slowly, we began swaying to "She's Out of My Life."

I didn't really know how to sway. I'd never done it before. But it came pretty naturally. And I could tell from the lyrics that the song was about losing a lover.

The song made me think of Aaban. Yet here I was dancing with Fatu. Not good.

Aaban seemed far away as Fatu whispered the lyrics in my ear. I could feel the warmth of her breath. In a strange way, I liked it. But I didn't like what it was doing to my conscience. Emotions darted in and out of my being—passion, exhilaration, sadness, joy, guilt, liberation, and pain.

Ultimately, betrayal trumped them all. I knew I was violating a trust. Aaban was obsessive when it came to me and other women. She didn't like me to socialize with other women. She'd be heartbroken if she knew I was dancing in the arms of another woman. And Fatu wasn't just any woman. She was Aaban's friend.

The urge to break away and run was overcome by my desire to stay put. I just liked the experience. It wasn't until the song ended that I realized that I was sweating. I stumbled off the dance floor and collapsed into a chair. Sitting there, I just couldn't square my mind with my heart. On one hand I felt I had double-crossed my family, my faith, and Aaban. Yet I liked how it felt to dance that way to that music. I couldn't lie to myself—I wanted to feel that sensation again.

I went home that night convinced that the devil had gotten hold of me.

The next morning I woke to the sound of my doorbell. I looked at the clock beside my bed: 7:30. I rolled over and closed my eyes. But the doorbell rang again. And then again. I dragged myself to the door.

"Who is it?"

"Me."

I unlocked the door and headed back to my bedroom. Aaban entered and followed me to my bed. "What is going on? Are you okay?"

"I'm just tired," I said impatiently, pulling a blanket over me and closing my eyes. "I got home very late."

She knelt down beside the bed and put her face next to mine, like she wanted a kiss. I heard her sniffing, like she was trying to detect alcohol on my breath.

"Are you a cat?" I said.

"It looks like it was a long, red night." *Red* was code for *partying*.

126

"It depends how you see it."

She plopped down on the bed.

"I want to sleep," I said. "Don't you have a lecture to attend?"

"Lectures can wait. I want to hear everything."

"I will tell you. But not now. I want to sleep."

"No. What you need is a strong tea."

Minutes later she returned to the room with a mug. "Here, drink this."

I rubbed my eyes and took sips between yawns.

"You danced too much, huh?" she said.

"Just a little."

"With whom?"

"A group I went with."

"Who is in the group?"

"Fatu, her brother, and some of their friends."

"Who did you dance with?"

"Just Fatu."

"How many times?"

"I can't remember."

"See? You danced so many times you can't remember how many."

"I just danced one song."

"Which song?"

"I can't remember."

"Was it a slow song?"

"Michael Jackson. One of his slow songs."

She grabbed my shoulders and started shaking me. "You danced slow with Fatu?"

I said nothing.

"What were the words to the song?"

"I can't remember."

"You can't remember?"

"Aaban, it was the first time I heard the song."

"How did she hold you? How did you hold her?"

I said nothing.

"When you were dancing with her, were you thinking of me?"

"Of course."

"Was she singing the song in your ear?"

"C'mon, Aaban."

"Did she put her head in your chest?"

"No!"

"You are lying!"

"I am not lying!"

"How can you have Fatu on your arm and be thinking of me?"

I rolled over and pounded my fist into my pillow.

Aaban started crying. "She betrayed me."

"Why the hell did I even go that place?" I said under my breath.

"Fatu betrayed me," she repeated, sobbing.

"Nothing happened," I shouted. "We just danced one time in front of everybody. It was nothing!"

Aaban sobbed.

"I could have lied and told you I didn't go there or that I didn't dance with her. I told you because I have nothing to hide."

Still no response.

"I have no feelings for Fatu. None."

Aaban never spoke to Fatu again. Their relationship was ruined. But she eventually forgave me. I knew that I had hurt her.

But something more profound had taken place at the Christmas party. My experience in the high-rise above the Nile opened my eyes to how powerful the pull of Western culture could be. I went there with apprehension, and I left there with guilt. Yet new desires and emotions had been stirred in me.

The notion that Western culture was evil had been drummed into me for so long, but the music had so much energy. I wanted to experience that sound and sensation again. The fact that this lifestyle was forbidden somehow drew me in.

TRANSFORMATION

I was a man who had never had the chance to be a boy. All my life, everything had been geared toward religious training. School was a means to becoming a cleric. Fun was simply forbidden. My only diversion was drawing, and I was beaten whenever I tried drawing at home. At college I had insulated myself from Cairo's rich nightlife scene, despite the fact that many Muslim students were going to clubs and parties where there were Western music and Western women.

Now that I had discovered what they had discovered, I wanted more.

A few months after the blowup with Aaban, I purchased a small stereo. It had a cassette deck, an amplifier, an equalizer, and two large speakers. I put it in my living room. I also picked up a copy of *Thriller*. One morning I had the *Thriller* cassette playing while I got dressed for school. Aaban showed up unexpectedly. She never dropped by on school mornings. She walked in on me when I was humming a tune.

"What's gotten into you, Awal?"

"What do you mean?"

"I see you shaking your head and your legs."

"So?"

"It means Fatu has succeeded. The devil's gang has drawn you into their fold."

"Now you are making me one of them? I've become a devil?"

"That's not what I mean. But you're headed in that direction."

"Is that why you showed up at my place so early in the morning? You thought you were going to find someone in my bed?"

"No. But if you are really in love, you should listen to Umm Kulthum."

"To me, Umm Kulthum sounds like funeral music."

"I can't believe you talk this way."

"I'm just saying I'd rather listen to Michael Jackson."

"You are a Muslim. How can you listen to Michael Jackson?"

"Many Muslims are listening to Michael Jackson."

"But you are not just *any* Muslim. You are studying to be a cleric. You have an image to uphold. And that kind of music taints your image and corrupts you in the process."

"But he's not saying anything bad. He's no different from Umm Kulthum. He's singing about love and life."

"Oh, Awal, how can you compare this guy to Umm?"

"Why don't you just sit down and listen to one of Jackson's songs?"

She didn't say anything.

"C'mon. I'll even give you the lyrics so you can see what he's saying. Then you can judge. He doesn't say anything dirty or evil."

"Try me," she said.

"I will."

I handed her the lyrics to "Billie Jean," and she read them.

"Anything wrong there? Anything you see that cannot be said inside a mosque?"

She finished reading the lyrics and set them down on the table. "He's evil."

"Oh! So because he's an American, he's evil?"

I knew I wasn't going to win the music argument with Aaban. So I gave up. But I kept buying more and more Western music from such artists as The Commodores; Prince; and Earth, Wind & Fire. It was as if I had caught an illness that I couldn't shake. The difference was that I didn't want to shake it.

Eventually, Aaban stopped hounding me, too. Then one day she dropped by when I was playing "Sail On." She stood and listened for a minute.

"Is this Michael Jackson, too?"

"No. The singer is Lionel Ritchie. The group is called The Commodores."

I handed her the record jacket.

"These are Sudanese?"

"No. They are American."

"I mean they are black," she said.

"Yes, of course. Can't you see?"

"Can you repeat the song?"

I played it again.

There was something about Ritchie's sound that crossed the boundaries Aaban had placed around Western music. By the time The Commodores reached the chorus, Aaban was swaying back and forth, unaware of what she was doing.

I just smiled. Whatever it was that had gotten into me was now into her.

"Can you play it again?" she said.

I did.

She turned down the lights and put her arms around me. It was a breakthrough.

But it was more than that. These songs had the ability to unite Africans and Arabs, Muslims and Christians, black people and white people. That's the lasting impression I took away from the Christmas Eve party I had gone to. Western pop music had erased the religious and cultural barriers that sharply divide the Arab world. The vibe on the dance floor was a sharp contrast to the harsh rhetoric being pounded into me in the Islamic studies program at Al-Azhar.

Aaban couldn't argue with any of this. But it made her nervous to think that we were going against everything we had been taught.

CHAPTER 15

PEOPLE ARE TALKING

Around the time that Aaban started experimenting with Western music, I was walking across the Al-Azhar campus one afternoon when I heard a man shout: "Infidels."

I stopped. The voice was coming from behind me, and I knew I recognized it from somewhere.

"Infidels," he said again. Only this time the voice was closer.

I spun around. It was Habib, my childhood friend who used to hang out with me under the neem tree next to my house, the one who hit the prostitute in the head for no reason.

"Sheik Habib!" I shouted.

"Momen."

We embraced. Then we stepped back and looked at each other. It had been a long time. When I went off to boarding school in Gashua, Habib's father had sent him to Iran to study. I never saw him after that, although I had heard through the grapevine that he had converted from Sunni Islam to Shia Islam and become much more militant in his thinking.

I could tell right away that this information was true. His pant legs were above his shoes. Shia Muslims believe that anything touching the ground—including trousers—can take in filth. And he was wearing an Iranian Sharia gown, an outward indication that he had embraced an extreme interpretation of Islamic law. Meantime, I was in jeans and a T-shirt. His expression was one of disapproval. Still, he was eager to catch up. We discussed family and old friends. But the conversation quickly turned to religion.

"Egypt *stinks* of Americanism," he said, launching into a tirade about the evils of the United States. "Egypt has sold out. It has Americanized."

I didn't share his view, but I decided not to argue with him. I certainly didn't mention that I had become a Michael Jackson fan.

"Mubarak is no better than Sadat," he continued. "He isn't going to bring Egypt back to being a Muslim state."

I kept listening.

"The Americans are giving him millions of dollars," he said. "But the Iranians and Saudis could have given him more."

"So why did you come to Egypt?" I asked.

"I came to study at Al-Azhar. But based on what I've seen, I can't stay."

"Where will you go?"

"Back to Iran."

"Didn't you know Egypt was this way before you got here?"

"No. But look at the way the women dress here. Look at all the Europeans and Americans walking naked on Egyptian streets. They should have destroyed those pyramids. Then these tourists would have no excuse to come here."

We were standing in the middle of the square on campus. Yet he was shouting. I could see the veins in his neck and his forehead.

"Mubarak is CIA," he said.

"That's what you think?"

"Sure. He's an agent for the American government. Saddam Hussein is a CIA agent too."

I found that absurd. But I saw no point in arguing about it.

"The problem is the Americans are working for the Israel state," he said. "And you can't trust Jews. They will use Saddam and Mubarak. Then later they will get rid of them."

I nodded, trying to hide the fact that I thought his conspiracy theory was crazy.

"But the Brotherhood will soon come to power. Jihad is going on underground. We will spring out soon. The righteous will rise high. You will see."

I never saw Habib after that brief encounter. Our paths just never crossed again. But it was strange to think that he and I used to sit on a carpenter's table under a tree in our little neighborhood and talk about Shakespeare and love stories. Not long before, we'd been kids. Somehow, he had grown into a man who was primed to carry out extreme violence to Jews and Americans. I guess there were early indicators. As a boy he had felt justified in bashing the head of a prostitute because prostitutes are evil. As an adult he decided Jews and Westerners were evil; therefore it was justifiable to bash them, too.

A couple of months after our encounter, I heard that he had withdrawn from Al-Azhar and moved back to Iran. Yet I ran into more Muslims on campus that sounded like Habib. They were embracing violent rhetoric toward the West. It was always justified by pointing out that Western music, movies, and fashion were an affront to Allah. Increasingly, the fundamentalist students were sounding like militants.

Meantime, the students who were embracing Western culture were peaceful. They were also a lot more upbeat in their outlook on life. Guys like my friend Abraham who had taken me to the party may have been ignoring some of the strict teachings of Islam, but he never uttered words of hate and violence.

By the summer 1984, I had started going to nightclubs and parties every week with a small group of friends. All of them were Muslims, and all of them were men. Aaban wasn't pleased. She was well aware of the Islamic custom that allowed men to go out but kept women at home. That didn't change the fact that she was jealous. She was afraid I'd meet other women.

She was right. The clubs were full of women. It became increasingly hard for me to resist the opportunities to dance with them and get somewhat involved with them. It happened gradually. Each night when I'd return home, Aaban would be waiting. She wanted to know every detail about whom I had been with and what I had done.

I kept assuring her that my heart was set on marrying her. But I couldn't hide the fact that I was flirting with other women, which became a bone of contention in our relationship.

Alcohol and women were a big part of the party scene. I told myself that I could resist the booze and stay true to Aaban. But my father was no longer around, and I didn't have the eyes of my village on me. At the same time, I was in an environment where virtually every man had a drink in one hand and a woman on his arm.

One evening I went with Abraham and some of his French friends to a rooftop party in Cairo. There were lots of students there, including college girls from Africa, Europe, and Latin America. I had never seen so many beautiful girls in one place.

"Would you like a beer?" one of my friends asked.

"No," I said.

Moments later another friend approached. "Want a beer?"

I noticed that everyone had a drink in their hand. I figured I wouldn't have to keep saying no if I had a glass in mine. So I reached for a glass of 7UP and took a gulp. It burned my throat and started coming up my nose. It was the hottest beverage I had ever swallowed. For a minute I felt like the room was spinning. I fell into a soft chair and stayed put until I felt better.

That's when a stunning girl from Madagascar approached. "What are you drinking?" she asked.

I handed her my glass. She smelled it. "Oh, gin," she said. "My favorite."

She took a sip from my glass and then sat on my lap. She had on a very short white dress with shoulder straps. When she sat down, I could see all the way up her legs to her underwear.

"What is your name?" she asked.

"Muhammad."

"I'm Jacqueline."

A waiter approached.

"Two gins," she told him.

I drank another gin while she stayed on my lap. I don't remember a lot of what happened after that, except that she stayed with me the rest of the evening and ordered more drinks. Some of my friends eventually took me home. My bed felt like it was spinning that night. I couldn't put my head on the pillow. I had never felt sicker in my life. The following day I slept until 4 p.m. I woke up with a splitting headache. The only reason I woke up then was that someone was ringing my doorbell. I was afraid it would be Aaban. But it was one of my classmates at Al-Azhar. His father was a powerful sheik back in Nigeria.

I stumbled to the door and let him in.

He took one look at me and asked, "What's your problem?"

"I went to this party and I drank a lot."

"What did you drink?"

"Uh, umm. Uh, that thing they call gin."

"You have a hangover."

"What do you mean by hangover?"

"When you drink a lot of alcohol in the night and wake up with a headache, that's a hangover."

"I wish it would go away."

"The only way to get rid of it is to have another drink."

"What do you mean, have another drink?"

"That's what you need to do."

"No way. It felt like my bed was running away from me."

"That's why I'm telling you that you need to drink another gin. Only this time you need to have lime with your gin."

"So you're telling me that if I drink gin again with lime I won't wake up with another hangover tomorrow?"

"That's right."

"I can't believe that."

He turned up his hands and smiled. "I'm telling you."

"This is how the devil works," I said. "He says, 'Come in. The water is not deep.' By the time you realize it, you are sinking down the drain. I won't go that way. Why can't I just take aspirin?"

"You can try. But it won't work. You need to come and have a drink."

I wasn't sure what to do. I showered and dressed, all the while thinking of something my father used to say: "Once you put one leg inside a place, you will follow with your other leg." "Never try alcohol," he'd tell me. "They will ask you to try. But when you try you are doomed."

As I left my apartment with my friend that evening, I felt like I was putting my other leg in. I was selling myself to Satan. That night I ended up in another bar, drinking gin with lime. The crazy thing is that my headache did go away.

I needed some new clothes. Once I started going to clubs and parties, I had to dress the part. That meant a return trip to Port Said. One of my friends took me there. It was my first time in a Western-style clothing store. The store had mirrors everywhere. And all the sales clerks were women, beautiful Egyptian girls.

"This would look good on you," one of them said to me. She handed me a T-shirt and a pair of blue jeans and led me to a dressing room. It had a mirror on the outside of the door. Once inside, I discovered a mirror on the inside of the door, too. Afraid that people could see through the glass, I quickly opened the door and stepped out to look through the mirror.

"What's the matter?" the sales woman said. "You don't like the clothes?"

I put my hands up. "No, no, no." Embarrassed, I stepped back inside and locked the door.

A few moments later, my friend started rapping on the door.

"What do you want?"

"How are the clothes?" he said.

I stepped out so he could see.

"Tuck in your shirt," he said.

"No way." In northern Nigeria we did not tuck in our shirts, and we did not wear belts. Both are insults to Allah. Instead of a belt we used rope, and it was hidden under our covers.

"You need to tuck it in," he said.

"Why?"

"People are looking at us."

Out of the corner of my eye I noticed the saleswoman. She had a grin on her face. I slipped back into the dressing room, closed the door, and tucked in my shirt. Then I looked in the mirror. Immediately I yanked the shirt out of my jeans.

"Did you do it?" my friend said through the door.

"Yes."

But when I opened the door, he saw that my shirt was still hanging down below my waistband.

"Why didn't you tuck it in like I told you?" he said.

"I did. But when I saw it in the mirror, I decided it looks okay not tucked in."

I was about to take the new clothes off so I could pay for them.

"No," he said. "They look good on you. Let's just go." He removed a pocketknife from his pants and cut the tags off my clothes. I paid for my new clothes, wrapped my old ones in a bag, and we left.

From that day forward I wore my traditional northern Nigerian clothing only when I returned home for visits. Even when I went to the mosque in Cairo, I wore a T-shirts and jeans. That's allowed in Egypt.

Aaban didn't like the changes she saw in me. When I replaced my wardrobe, she figured I was losing interest in the clergy.

"When you go home, what are you going to tell your family?" Aaban asked.

"I'm not going to tell them anything," I said.

"You are playing with fire."

"I know what I'm doing. It's not what you're thinking."

"You are like a horse that has lost its bridle," she said. "A horse without a bridle destroys himself and his rider. That's what you are doing to us."

My drinking worried her a lot more than my clothes. It got to a point where I'd meet up with my buddies every Thursday night to drink gin and go to the clubs. We called it gin night. There were five of us, and we'd each buy one bottle of gin. We smoked a lot, too. I didn't even like cigarettes. At least not at first. But the more I smoked, the more I was hooked.

I tried not to smoke around Aaban, but she knew I was doing it. She could smell it on my clothes and on my breath. Eventually I stopped trying to conceal it from her. There was no point. Besides, I was spending less time with her and more time at nightclubs with my friends. I even got a part-time job as a disc jockey at one club.

Shortly after I started working as a DJ, I acquired two roommates. Both guys were foreign students at Cairo University, where they were studying Arabic. I let them move in because I needed

help with the rent. I was spending a lot more money on liquor, cigarettes, clothing, and music.

One day I had agreed to meet up with my roommates at a
lounge near our apartment. I brought Aaban along because I hadn't
been spending much time with her. After Aaban and I arrived,
my two roommates showed up with three Italian girls. They were
young and stylishly dressed. Their features were striking—dark hair,
tanned skin, and thin figures. Aaban looked out of place in her traditional Muslim dress. Two of the girls seemed to be with my two
roommates. The third woman was just tagging along. Her name was
Ilaria Alphi.

Aaban immediately did the math and assumed Ilaria was there
to hook up with me. "I had no idea my roommates were bringing
girls," I told her when we got home that night, insisting I had no
interest in those girls. They were complete strangers.

But the truth was that Ilaria intrigued me. In the brief time we
were together in the lounge that evening, I could see that she was
witty, clever, and well educated. She had been all over Europe. My
attraction to her wasn't romantic. She just seemed so interesting.
I wanted to ask her all kinds of questions. But I didn't dare with
Aaban beside me.

I did run into her a couple of times at the club where I worked,
however. All we did was talk. Still, Aaban was deeply suspicious.
One morning about six months after I began working at the nightclub, Aaban woke me up by knocking on my door at dawn. I had
been drinking a lot the night before and hadn't gotten into bed
until after three.

When I opened the door to let her in, she immediately started
crying.

"Why are you crying?" I asked.

She said nothing.

"Can you give me one reason for your crying?"

Without answering, she went around the house like she was

looking for something. She picked up a glass on the kitchen counter, inspecting it for lipstick marks.

"Nothing is going on," I said.

She put the glass down and headed into my bedroom.

"You are supposed to trust me," I said, trailing her. "And you don't."

"I trust you," she said. "But I don't trust those girls, and I don't trust your friends."

"If you say you trust me, you have to show that you trust me."

"That's why I don't want you working at that club. The friends you are meeting there are getting between us."

"What do you mean?"

"I mean we used to be happy. Now we are always arguing."

Shortly after I met Ilaria she left Cairo, and I lost track of her. My two roommates moved out, too. That made Aaban happy. At the same time, my reputation as a DJ was spreading. People were starting to request me to work private parties. I was even getting requests from diplomats and Egyptian businessmen. That eventually led to a full-time position as the in-house DJ at a five-star hotel near the Egyptian pyramids.

All the attention made me feel important. For the first time in my adult life, I began to think seriously about doing something other than joining the clergy. I still believed in Islam. I continued to follow the rituals. But I was becoming less orthodox. And I was spending a lot less time at the mosque. I still read the Qur'an daily, but its influence was being eclipsed by pop music. The bottom line was that I was praying less and partying more. A lot more. Yet, I was making good progress toward my PhD in Islamic studies.

Then at the end of 1985 I made a quick trip home to Nigeria to visit my family. I don't remember precisely when it was. But I made the mistake of flying to Nigeria in a pair of blue jeans and a collared shirt. When my mother first laid eyes on me, she covered her mouth with her hand. My father practically knocked her down in his rush to get in my face.

"You are walking naked," he shouted.

The top two buttons on my shirt were undone, enabling him to see the upper portion of my chest. He stormed out in disgust. My father was all about image and shame. Those two things seemed to matter to him more than anything else.

It didn't take long for word to spread through the village that I was dressed immodestly. Within a couple of days my father was hearing it from his friends at the mosque. Then I started hearing it from my father.

"People are talking," he shouted at me.

That expression spelled trouble. It meant that people were whispering amongst themselves, complaining that I was dressing like a pagan instead of an aspiring cleric. I was supposed to be a model for the younger boys. Instead, my father felt that I was flaunting my rebellious ways.

It was all gossip. I wasn't flaunting. But I had certainly been careless in not hiding my new wardrobe. If I had been thinking, I would have left my Western clothes behind at my apartment in Cairo. The last thing I wanted to do was rile up my father.

None of that mattered now. What mattered in my home village was the talk on the street. Especially to my father. My dress had embarrassed him. I had brought dishonor to the family. And in my father's book, insults to honor were offenses of the highest order.

There had been more than one instance in northern Nigeria of a father killing a child who had brought dishonor to the family by disregarding the teachings of Islam. So when my father complained that people were talking, I understood those to be words of peril.

Needless to say, I kept quiet about my new job as a nightclub DJ, the alcohol, the smoking, and the rest. Nor did I let on that my

142

plans of becoming a cleric had cooled. But my father had his own suspicions about my worthiness. Between the camera incident and the change in clothing, he cut off all conversation with me. Still, while I was home, I made a point of attending the mosque. And I went out of my way to make sure my father saw me praying frequently and participating in all the rituals.

I couldn't wait to get back to Cairo, though. The whole time I was home, I was thinking that Nigeria was no longer my home. Egypt was my home. I fit in better there.

CHAPTER 16

HIGHER EDUCATION

Early in 1986, my friend Abraham asked if he could move in with me. He promised it would only be temporary while he looked for a new apartment. On his second night at my place, he showed up with a bottle of vodka and two girls from Somalia. One of them was holding onto Abraham's arm, like a girlfriend. The other one was the most exotic-looking woman I had ever laid eyes on. Her name was Fatima. She had on an extremely low-cut, skintight, gray dress with sequins. The silk fabric was so thin I could see her voluptuous body. I felt guilty just looking at her.

Fatima came from a very wealthy family. Her father was a powerful man of influence in politics, and she had studied in India before transferring to a college in Cairo. Abraham told me that she was a big drinker and had a wild streak. I sensed she was trouble. Yet I found her fascinating and hard to look away from.

After the four of us drank a round of shots, we went to a disco near the pyramids. Shortly after we arrived, Fatima led me to the dance floor. All the men were staring at her. In a club full of young, beautiful women, Fatima was in a class of her own. I'd never seen a woman so seductive. She danced that way, too, undoing my top shirt buttons and running her hands over my chest as she gyrated provocatively. It was so physical and aggressive it made me uncomfortable.

"Stop doing that," I told her.

She laughed and kept going, creating a spectacle. Despite being ashamed, I was mesmerized by the most beautiful woman in the entire nightclub.

Afterward, the four of us returned to my apartment. On the way, we picked up another bottle of vodka. After downing a few more shots, Abraham put on "Sexual Healing," by Marvin Gaye. Then he retired to his bedroom with his girlfriend. That left me alone with Fatima. I wasn't sure what to do next. As provocative as she looked, I wasn't about to take her to my bedroom.

Standing in my living room, Fatima unfastened her bra. "Look at me," she shouted. "I'm beau-u-utiful. I'm y-y-y-young. And I'm r-r-r-rich."

I froze. I had never had sex before. Not even with Aaban.

"What's your problem?" she said.

"You are my problem."

She marched down the hallway and banged on Abraham's door. "What do you want?" he yelled.

"This idiot doesn't want to do anything," she told him. "Are we in a mosque?"

Abraham opened the door and tried to calm her down.

"You brought me here to him," she told him. "I should have gone with someone else."

Abraham gave me the evil eye. "You should take care of your own problem," he told me. Then he closed his bedroom door.

Fatima walked back toward me. Her demeanor changed. "I'm sorry," she said. "You are a nice man."

"And you are a beautiful woman," I told her.

She appreciated the compliment, and I was glad she had calmed down.

"Let's go to sleep," she said.

"You go in my bedroom and take the bed," I told her. "I'll sleep on the couch."

"I'll sleep wherever you sleep," she said.

Then she removed her clothing. Previously, the only naked women I'd seen were in the bush in Africa. Fatima looked like she belonged in a magazine. She had golden brown skin, a flat stomach, and curves everywhere else. I was utterly powerless to look away. My heart raced. My palms got sweaty. Guilt told me to resist. Smoking and drinking and wearing Western clothes were one thing. But having sex with a woman was another thing altogether. In Islam, having sex outside marriage is right behind murder in seriousness. People are stoned to death for it.

But when she pressed up against me and started kissing me, I could not resist.

The next morning I woke up with Fatima in my bed. We reeked of alcohol. And it was the Sabbath. I had already missed morning prayer. I shut my eyes and thought of Aaban. We'd been together for nearly three years. Yet we'd never slept together. Aaban was still a virgin, saving herself for when we were married.

I had never felt so low. Here I was lying beside the most exotic woman I'd ever encountered. Yet I felt sick inside. I rubbed my eyes violently, hoping I could wake up and discover this had all been a nightmare. But it had really happened. I was stuck with a sort of guilt like I had never felt before. I literally had trouble breathing, as if someone had his hand around my throat. I hated myself.

How will I tell Aaban? I wondered. She had a tendency to become hysterical if I simply danced with another woman. If I told her what I'd done with Fatima, I feared she might commit suicide. I decided not to tell her anything. I wouldn't even mention Fatima.

I cut off all contact with Fatima. She kept trying to phone me, but I never returned her calls. After a month, the calls finally stopped. Abraham had moved out, and I had stopped going to parties unless I was with Aaban. More than anything, I wanted to marry her and spend the rest of my life with her. I was harboring a secret. But I kept telling myself it was better not to break her heart.

Partway through the spring semester in 1986, I accompanied Aaban to a party that was hosted by a wealthy family from Sudan. The family had ties to royalty, and Aaban's father had been invited to attend because of his role with the Arab League. The party was held at a stately home in Cairo. Most of the guests were older and much, much wealthier.

At one point, I was on a sofa in a sitting room. Aaban was standing on the opposite side of the room, mingling with a group of older, distinguished women who were friends of her family. Bored, I looked up and saw Fatima heading straight toward me. "You," she screamed, as she jumped in my lap.

All eyes were on Fatima. She was wearing a halter top made with very little fabric. She wrapped her arms around my neck. "I've been looking for you since that night," she said.

Her voice was loud, and I could smell alcohol on her breath.

"Fatima, that's enough," I said, pushing her off my lap.

"You can't do that to me," she said.

I could feel Aaban's eyes on me.

"Fatima," I said.

"You are beautiful and handsome," she said, caressing the side of my face with her hand.

I pushed her hand away.

"I thought you were better than all those Nigerians," she said. "But you are the same."

Aaban stepped forward. "What is all this scandal?" she said.

"Aaban, this woman is drunk!" I snapped.

"This is the result of your nightlife," Aaban said.

Angry, Fatima grabbed Aaban by the collar and yanked her back, snapping the necklace around Aaban's neck. Instantly, a family friend jumped to Aaban's aid, pushing Fatima away. A large Somali who had showed up with Fatima grabbed the man who had aided Aaban, throwing him to the ground. Then the Somali grabbed me by the shoulders and pushed me through an open window in the parlor. I landed on a porch. A brawl ensued. People got hurt. Furniture got broken. And the party ended in disgrace.

For the next two weeks, Aaban refused to see me. I finally cornered her by waiting outside her apartment one evening. "We need to talk," I told her.

"I don't want to talk."

"Aaban, please."

"You have made a choice. Drinking and all that. And now this woman from Somalia. Fatima."

"You are making things difficult for me," I said.

She laughed. "You have nobody to blame but yourself. When you are doing those things, you are enjoying yourself. But you are not thinking that a day like this will come."

"I'm sorry, Aaban."

"So this is what you've been doing all these nights? You've been sleeping with Fatima."

"I'm sorry."

She started crying.

I patted her shoulder at first. Then I wrapped my arms around her. She buried her head in my shoulder and wept. I felt lower than dirt. "I'm so sorry, Aaban. So sorry."

We sat down, and I held her for nearly an hour. Neither of us said a word. I cried the entire time. So did she. Finally, she stood. "You have to promise me one thing," she said. "I will forgive you.

But I never want to hear that woman's name spoken again. And I never want you to so much as speak to her. Ever!"

"I will do that," I said.

"Now, I have to go."

"I will walk you downstairs," I said.

"No. You just stay here. I need some time alone."

I watched her walk down the circular staircase. When she reached the ground, she looked up at me, kissed her hand, and waved good-bye.

I spent months trying to regain Aaban's trust. During that time I drank more than ever. It got to a point where Aaban urged me to attend AA meetings. I did for a while. But I stopped after a few sessions. My addiction placed another layer of stress on my relationship with Aaban. It also distracted me from completing my thesis for my degree in Islamic studies. My topic was the historical origins of Islam. The research led me to probe the prophet Muhammad's background and his lifestyle. That line of inquiry ultimately led me to the prophet's nine wives.

Polygamy wasn't a new concept to me. I had grown up with it in Nigeria. As far back as primary school, I had learned a song called "Muhammad's Wives." All nine of the prophet's wives were named in the song.

Such early exposure to the concept of plural marriage had caused me to accept the practice. Everyone in my village had been raised to believe that Allah accepted polygamy. Naturally, most of the men in my village had multiple wives.

But my thesis research introduced me to some books that cast the prophet Muhammad in a less favorable light. Under Islamic law, books that question the legitimacy of the prophet Muhammad are strictly forbidden. Simply possessing a book of that nature was considered worse than having pornography. Both distributors and consumers were at risk of severe persecution and even death under some interpretations of Islamic law. The only way to get books like this was through underground booksellers. I got my hands on a few through an acquaintance at the disco where I worked. The acquaintance was from Senegal, and he had access to underground booksellers.

I pored through the books in the privacy of my apartment. They contained information on one of the prophet Muhammad's wives known widely as Mary the Coptic Maid. Around A.D. 630 the governor of Egypt sent Mary and her sister Shirin to Muhammad as gifts. Mary is described as "comely" and possessing a "fair complexion and delicate features" that "fascinated the heart of Muhammad." Muhammad added Mary to his harem and offered Mary's sister to one of his servants.

I made sure not to let anyone see what I was reading. Not even Aaban. I kept the books hidden behind a heater in my bathroom.

But I had a harder time hiding my thoughts. The realization that the prophet of Islam had taken a Christian servant as a polygamous wife didn't sit well with me. I could not come to grips with the idea that a prophet with so many wives needed yet another wife, especially a beautiful young Christian, added to his harem.

The further I dug for answers, the more disenchanted I became with the whole situation. Eventually, I started to question the legitimacy of Muhammad being a prophet.

And if he wasn't a prophet, then the whole idea of Islam was a fraud.

That wasn't the sort of idea a student at Al-Azhar should have been entertaining.

If my true feelings ever got out, I'd be seen as blasphemous. My personal safety would be at risk. So rather than talk to anybody, I put my private thoughts down on paper.

The professor overseeing my thesis had been pressing me to complete the project. He was a tall, robust man with neatly cropped, smooth brown hair. His mustache was neatly trimmed, and his beard, with its long strands of gray, signified his membership in the Society of the Muslim Brothers. He also had the mark of the coin on his forehead. It's a mark of piety that is the result of bowing down in ritual prayers and pressing one's forehead against the floor. My father had the same mark on his forehead. To obtain the mark of the coin, a man must go well beyond the required five prayers per day.

At the beginning of the summer of 1985, my professor summoned me to his office, a large room with framed verses from the Qur'an hanging on all four walls. When I arrived, he had on a black jacket over a white flowing gown with white trousers. He sat behind a large wooden table topped with books, papers, and wooden penholders. I sat opposite him.

"I haven't seen you for a while," he began. "And now you are behind."

"Yes. I have been doing a lot of extra research," I said.

"So where are your papers?"

"I'm not finished yet."

"Let me see your papers."

Trying not to appear nervous, I reached into my leather bag and removed my notepad. He put out his hand and I gave it to him. He started flipping through the pages.

"What is this I'm reading?" He looked captivated as he turned from page to page.

Proud, I said nothing.

"Did you write this?" he finally said.

"Yes."

"Are you sure you wrote this?"

"Yes."

"Anybody help you write this?"

"No."

"Are you sure you didn't work with somebody?"

"Yes, I'm sure."

He shook his head while his face registered a look of disgust.

My heart skipped a beat. Had I accidentally handed him the wrong notepad?

He shook my notepad in his hand. "Have you showed this to anyone else?"

"No."

"Are you sure nobody has seen this?"

"Nobody."

He tore the pages from my notepad, crumpled them into a ball, and rose to his feet. Then he shook his fist at me. "This," he said in a hushed tone, "can never be seen by anyone."

Somehow, I had mistakenly handed him my personal notes instead of my thesis draft.

He slammed his fist on his desk. "These must be burned to ashes," he thundered.

Frightened, I said nothing.

"Do you have more pages like this?" he asked.

"No."

"There is no other copy?"

There was no way I was going to admit that I had carbon copies of my notes back at my apartment. They were hidden with my underground books behind the heater in my bathroom.

He paced back and forth behind his desk. Then he came out from behind the desk and wagged his finger in my face. "I don't ever want to hear about this again. Never, ever discuss this with anybody. Not even in your dreams."

I nodded my head up and down.

"Now get out," he shouted, pointing to the door. "Out!"

I grabbed my bag and scurried toward the door.

"You're making your blood eligible for shedding," he said. "Whoever kills you will go to paradise."

Anxious to destroy the other papers, I rushed directly from campus to my apartment. I was surprised to find Aaban there waiting for me. She could tell from the look on my face that something was terribly wrong.

"What is it?" she asked.

Without saying a word, I brushed past her and into the bathroom. A few minutes later I emerged with the carbon copies of my papers.

"What's that?" she asked.

"My thesis has been rejected."

"So come up with another topic."

"It's not that simple."

"I don't understand," she said.

I handed her my notes.

There was a long, awkward silence while she read them. Then her eyes welled up and she started panting. The petrified expression on her face made me sick to my stomach. Finally she looked up.

"Do you know what you have done to us?" she asked.

"I'm sorry. I didn't mean for—"

"Did you ever think of me or your love for me or our dreams before writing such abominable things?"

"I know I—"

"What about your own life?" she continued.

Aaban became hysterical, unable to come to grips with the fact that I had serious questions about the legitimacy of Islam. Those were incredibly dangerous thoughts, capable not only of getting a man in my shoes killed but also threatening the safety of those closest to me.

"We're as good as dead!" she cried. "You have called down the wrath and vengeance of the Almighty!"

I knew she was right. Tears streamed down my face.

"What was your intention?" she shouted.

I didn't know what to say. I felt too humiliated to answer.

Aaban fell back on the couch. She couldn't believe that I had made it out of my professor's office in one piece. "You should thank the Almighty for that," she said. "You've done the worst sin one could ever do."

"I know," I cried.

"You've lost me," she said.

It took me a minute to grasp what she was saying. Then I pleaded with her not to leave me. The prospect of losing her made me frantic. Suddenly I lost all feeling in my legs. I collapsed on the floor.

Aaban screamed, dropped to her knees, and tried to aid me. Before I knew it, we were in each other's arms. We knew we had to stick together. We were in this mess together.

Aaban insisted that I had to get out of Egypt at once. I agreed. But where would I go? Home wasn't an option.

She suggested Sudan. Her sisters were there. Aaban said I could live with them until the danger subsided.

Over the next week, I became paralyzed by paranoia. I felt like everyone was watching me. If someone made eye contact with me, I looked away. When someone sat next to me on the metro train, I moved. One afternoon a close friend sneaked up behind me at a bus stop and put his hands on my shoulders. I nearly jumped out of my skin.

I had become so fearful of being hauled in for blasphemy that I lost my appetite and was suffering from insomnia. In a week's time I lost over ten pounds and had bags under my bloodshot eyes.

It was going to take some time to get the paperwork processed for me to go to Sudan. Another problem was that if I withdrew from school, I'd have to face the wrath of my father and the village elders back home. I had already escaped severe punishment before one tribunal in my hometown. No doubt the outcome would not be so favorable the second time. There would be zero tolerance for writing blasphemous thoughts about the prophet of Islam, no matter how private. My father would see to that.

I felt trapped. There was just no way out of my predicament.

A little over a week after my encounter with my professor, I went with two friends to take a colleague to the airport. On the way back, our vehicle was accidentally run off the road by a truck, causing our car to roll over numerous times. The driver was killed instantly. My other friend, who was seated in the passenger seat, broke both of his legs. I was in the back seat and escaped with the least serious injuries—a broken arm and multiple lacerations and bruises about my head, face, and legs. Although my injuries were not life threatening, my arm sustained a clean break above the bicep. It was serious enough that Al-Azhar granted me a one-semester deferment while I went home for medical treatment. Ultimately, I ended up seeing a surgeon in Italy before undergoing eight weeks of rehabilitation back in Nigeria.

The eight weeks away from Al-Azhar and Cairo were a relief. In addition to providing a valid excuse for being out of school, the accident gave me time to figure out my next move. The accident also cemented my relationship with Aaban, even though she remained in Cairo while I underwent medical treatment in Italy and rehab back home. It was the first time we had been apart for such an extended period of time.

CHAPTER 17

WHAT RELIGION IS THIS?

When I finally returned to Cairo, Aaban was waiting for me at the airport. We threw our arms around each other. "I missed you so much," she said.

"I missed you, too, Aaban. I hope you are a little more relaxed now."

"I am. But I'm worried."

"My arm is well now. I went to Italy, and the doctor said it will heal. I'm young."

"But we still don't know what's going to happen to you with the school. And if this thing explodes, we will be torn apart." She started crying.

"Why are you crying?"

"I've heard that you've been expelled from Al-Azhar," she said.

"What?"

"I don't know if it's true. But that's what I've been told."

Over the next couple of days I ran into a few of my classmates. They too had heard that I had been expelled from the school. I wasn't surprised. It was just odd that I hadn't received any sort of formal notice. Nonetheless, I had no intention of returning to campus. My days at Al-Azhar were over the moment my notes accidentally ended up in the hands of my professor. My bigger concern at the moment was my father. It wouldn't be long before word reached him that I'd been expelled. At that moment I'd be disowned.

Right away I went looking for a job. I met a foreign journalist from Holland. He called himself Dutch, and he hired me to translate for him. Dutch was relatively new to Egypt and was assigned to the Cairo bureau of his country's leading newspaper. But he couldn't speak any Arabic.

Dutch lived in an apartment building that housed many foreign correspondents from around the world. After I had been translating for him for a couple of months, he learned that I had fallen behind on my rent. We had become pretty good friends by then, and he invited me to move in with him.

Desperate for all the help I could get and eager to get as far away from Al-Azhar as possible, I accepted Dutch's offer. Aaban wasn't thrilled. The first time she visited me at Dutch's place, she sensed trouble. Dutch was a big drinker, and there were liquor bottles all over his place.

She was right. Dutch and I drank together often. He even nicknamed me "Drink and Die." He called me that because I'd drink so much gin that I'd pass out.

But drinking wasn't the biggest threat to my relationship with Aaban. A lot of foreign journalists lived in Dutch's apartment complex and the surrounding neighborhood. They were all friends and often hung out together. Not long after I moved into Dutch's place, he took me to a party with his friends. I was stunned to bump into Ilaria Alpi there. It had been close to two years since she left Cairo. But she had returned as a reporter for Radio Roma.

It wasn't as if she and I had had much of a relationship during her previous time in Cairo. We'd only been around each other a few times at parties. But there was a connection. Not necessarily a romantic one. I'm not saying there was no physical attraction. There was. But we thoroughly enjoyed talking to each other. After running into each other at the foreign journalists' party, we agreed to meet up the next night for drinks at a local pub. We drank a lot that night and ended up talking until well after midnight. Then she invited me back to her place.

Ilaria lived with three other single women. They were all from Rome. They were all beautiful. And their attitudes toward sex were much more liberal than anything I had encountered. When I arrived at Ilaria's place, her roommates were walking around in nothing but their underwear. It didn't seem to bother them that a man was in the apartment.

It was late, and Ilaria took me into her bedroom. I relaxed on the bed while she took a shower. When she emerged from the bathroom, she was naked. Yet she wasn't coming on to me. That's just the way she was. Then she invited me to share her bed for the night.

I did, though we didn't have sex that night. But we slept together numerous times without having sex. She never asked me about Aaban or any other women. She was free spirited and just saw me as a great friend. I saw her that way, too, albeit a beautiful one.

I never told Aaban about Ilaria. On one hand I felt pretty guilty about having that relationship behind her back. We were, after all, still planning to marry. That's why I knew I had to stop hanging around with Ilaria. At some point our friendship was going to destroy my relationship with Aaban. I pulled back.

Ilaria left Cairo on a journalism assignment. I never saw her after that. Then I learned that she was murdered on March 20, 1994, in Mogadishu, Somalia. She had been there working on a story. Today there is an investigative journalism award in her name.

One of the great things about living with Dutch was that he

didn't charge me any rent. In addition to translating for him, I started taking part-time classes at another university in Cairo. Plus, my part-time job as a DJ turned into a full-time one. I found myself getting more and more involved with pop music.

One evening in 1988 I went to visit an acquaintance named Gaston. He had been a frequent patron at the nightclub where I worked, and he invited me over to his house to record some music.

As soon as I arrived at Gaston's place, I removed a pack of cigarettes from my pocket. Remembering how much Gaston liked to smoke, I offered him a cigarette.

"I don't smoke anymore," Gaston said.

"Why not?" I asked.

Gaston didn't reply.

"Is it for religious reasons or for health reasons?" I persisted.

"Religion," Gaston said.

I laughed. At the club, Gaston had been practically a chain smoker.

I took a drag on my cigarette.

"Please smoke outside," Gaston said.

It was clear from his tone that he wasn't joking. I stepped outside to finish my cigarette. When I stepped back inside a few minutes later, he asked me if I wanted something to drink.

"I'll take a beer."

"I have no beer."

"Whiskey?"

"No whiskey, either."

"Any alcohol will do."

"I have no alcohol."

"Do you mean that you don't drink anymore?"

"Yes."

I found this hard to believe. I had never seen Gaston at the club without a drink in his hand.

"Don't tell me this is because of religion also."

"Yes."

"This is serious. What religion is this?"

"Christianity," Gaston said.

"Christianity?"

Gaston nodded.

I was far from an expert on Christianity. My understanding of its teachings was pretty superficial. Still, I had gone to school with Christians in Nigeria, and I had acquaintances in Cairo who were Christians. None of them had ever said that Christianity prohibited the consumption of alcohol and tobacco. So I was skeptical. I wanted written proof. I asked Gaston if these prohibitions were written in the Christian scriptures.

Before answering, he explained that not all Christians abstain from liquor and cigarettes. But, he continued, The Church of Jesus Christ of Latter-day Saints teaches that these things should be avoided because they are addictive.

I had never heard of The Church of Jesus Christ of Latter-day Saints.

Gaston said the Church is often referred to by its nickname—the Mormon church.

I had never heard the term *Mormon*, either. But the fact that a Christian faith prohibited the use of alcohol and cigarettes intrigued me. The Qur'an is silent on the subject of cigarettes, but it prohibits alcohol consumption. Yet I knew plenty of Muslims who drank.

I asked Gaston if there was anything written in Christian scripture that specifically forbade addictive substances.

Gaston nodded his head affirmatively.

I wanted to see it.

Gaston went to the bookshelf and returned with a book that he had opened to a specific page. He handed it to me and directed my eyes to a particular passage titled "A Word of Wisdom."

I started reading: "To be sent greeting; not by commandment or constraint, but by revelation and the word of wisdom, showing forth the order and will of God in the temporal salvation of all saints in the last days—given for a principle with promise, adapted to the capacity of the weak and the weakest of all saints, who are or can be called saints."

The tone immediately struck me. A word like *greeting* felt a lot more inviting than *commandment*. The Qur'an had always been taught to me in a harsh form—*thou shalt* do this and *thou shalt not* do that. But this passage felt more like a recommendation. I read on: "Inasmuch as any man drinketh wine or strong drink among you, behold it is not good. . . . And, again, tobacco is not for the body . . . and is not good for man."

The words were so straightforward—alcohol and tobacco are not good for the body and therefore should be avoided. I couldn't argue with that. Intrigued, I looked at the cover of the book. It said: The Book of Mormon: Another Testament of Jesus Christ. Under that was another title: The Doctrine & Covenants. It looked to me like two books in one. I looked up at Gaston. "Isn't this supposed to be the Bible?"

"This is scripture," Gaston said. "It's another testament of Jesus Christ."

"Testament? What do you mean by testament?"

Testament, Gaston explained, is a statement of beliefs. The Bible, made up of the Old and New Testaments, represents the testimony of the Jews. The Book of Mormon contains the testimony of the early inhabitants of the Americas.

Gaston said that the ancient people portrayed in the Book of Mormon migrated out of Jerusalem some six hundred years before the birth of Christ.

"So which church is this?" I asked.

The Church of Jesus Christ of Latter-day Saints, Gaston told me. The term *Mormon*, he explained, stems from the fact that Latter-day Saints view the Book of Mormon as scripture. Other Christian denominations do not.

I was about to light up another cigarette. But I thought better of it. Instead, I sat there taking it all in. Gaston had given me a lot to think about. Most of all, I couldn't get over the fact that Gaston had given up smoking and drinking. That alone made me want to know more about this unusual religion.

"When do you worship?" I asked.

"Fridays," he said.

I laughed. This was too much. Friday is a holy day for Muslims, not Christians.

Gaston explained that throughout most of the world, members of The Church of Jesus Christ of Latter-day Saints treat Sunday as the Sabbath. In Egypt, however, the church recognizes the Egyptian Sabbath, which is Friday. That puts the church in keeping with the customs of the country. It's a practical approach that enables Latter-day Saints to honor their obligations to their employers, all of whom are open for business on Sundays while being closed for religious observance on Fridays.

I couldn't get over the fact that Gaston had suddenly gone sober and was unwilling to touch cigarettes. It was a peculiar turn of events. I asked if I could visit the church.

Gaston said he'd be happy to accompany me.

I wondered if people would be angry over a Muslim visiting the church.

He told me not to worry. The congregation, he insisted, would welcome me.

This response was peculiar, too. I had been raised to believe that all Christian churches were evil. From as far back as I could remember, I had been taught that I shouldn't even look in the direction of a Christian church, let alone go inside one. My father would tell me that the God of Islam was a God that I needed to appease. Otherwise, Allah would rage.

Christians were heathens. Yet in my eyes, Gaston was anything but evil. I was curious to check out his new church.

CHAPTER 18

I WANT TO SEE

It was four o'clock on a Friday morning when I finished up my disc jockey work at the club in Cairo. By the time I cleaned up, ate, and commuted across the city, I arrived at Gaston's apartment just before seven. A bit nervous, I rang the bell.

Gaston was surprised to see me. "I didn't think you'd come," he said as he motioned for me to step inside.

But I had promised him I would show up. When I give someone my word, I follow through. Besides, I took it very seriously that he had converted to a new religion.

Gaston agreed that the transformation he had made was quite serious.

He also understood the significance of my standing on his doorstep. Orthodox Muslims consider it an act of apostasy to enter a Christian house of worship, and Islamic law spells out extreme punishment for apostasy. Gaston knew the stakes for me were high.

He also doubted whether I would be up for attending church after working at a nightclub until the early hours of the morning. Normally when I worked I drank a lot. It was pretty common for DJs to be sloshed by the end of the night. But Gaston could tell that I hadn't had a drink all night. That convinced him I was serious.

After giving me a quick primer on what to expect at church, Gaston hailed a taxi, and we headed toward a suburb of Cairo. He told me to expect to see a lot of Westerners in the congregation. Many of the church's members were Americans who worked in Egypt. There were very few native Egyptians in the congregation, although a number of Africans from other Christian denominations had joined the church.

All of this intrigued me. It just sounded so different from my experience as a Muslim. The mosques I had attended would never have accepted such a diverse collection of outsiders.

Once we were within about a block of the church, my heart started racing. *I'm going to church,* I thought. *Am I crazy?*

But my anxiety quickly disappeared the moment we arrived. I was looking for a church building or a cathedral. Instead, I was looking at a building in a residential neighborhood.

"Where's the church?" I asked.

"This is it," Gaston replied.

Very strange.

Gaston explained why his congregation didn't meet in a more traditional church facility—the Egyptian government still hadn't officially recognized The Church of Jesus Christ of Latter-day Saints. In addition to not having a building, church members were not allowed to proselytize, a condition that the members strictly observed.

I asked if it was okay for me to ask questions once inside.

He assured me that questions were fine.

This was strange, too. As a Muslim, I had been taught not to ask questions.

"Can I ask *any* question?"

"Any question you want to ask," Gaston told me.

"Are you sure?"

Gaston smiled. "I'm sure."

As soon as we entered the gate, a church member ushered us into the building. We walked through a doorway that led to a large room where church members were mingling. One of the first things I noticed was a sign on the bulletin board in the entrance. It strictly prohibited Latter-day Saints from proselytizing Egyptians or Muslims.

As Gaston had predicted, almost all of the church members mingling in that large room were Americans, along with a handful of Africans. Suddenly, I spotted someone I knew. Justice was an African native from Ghana who was teaching English at a Pakistani school in Cairo. He lived in my neighborhood and on a number of occasions we had drunk together and attended social parties.

Like Gaston, Justice had been a regular at the clubs, a guy who regularly drank and smoked. Yet here he was at a church that doesn't believe in drinking and smoking. I approached him.

"Justice, what are *you* doing here?"

"What are *you* doing here?" he asked.

I told him I was visiting.

He grinned and put his arms around me. Then he told me he had joined the church.

"What?"

Justice grinned and nodded.

At 9:30 sharp the congregation assembled and started singing a Christian hymn. The tune was unfamiliar. So were the words. Yet as I listened to the references to Christ and love, I felt as if wind were rushing through me. My heartbeat picked up as I observed the facial expressions of those around me. What I saw didn't match all the awful things I had been taught about Christians.

Gaston explained that it was customary on the first Sunday of each month for random members to stand up and testify from the podium. One after another, men and women of various races and nationalities expressed their faith in the divinity of Jesus Christ, along with their belief in the Bible and the Book of Mormon as holy scripture. A couple of the men who spoke were individuals I had seen in an intoxicated state at the clubs. To see them sober and singing praises to Christ had me scratching my head. Something was going on. I wasn't sure what. But I couldn't escape the feeling I had inside. I recognized that there had to be something to this Christian religion.

It was peculiar enough to see people who weren't clergy speaking from the podium. But then a little boy from Nigeria stood and walked to the podium. He could not have been older than nine or ten. He had on a white shirt and a tie and was barely tall enough to reach the microphone.

"Good morning, fathers and mothers," he said.

"Good morning!" the entire congregation responded.

"I am grateful to share my testimony," the boy said. "I love my family. I love everybody in the church. I am thankful for all the support I get from the church. The Book of Mormon is true. Joseph Smith is a prophet of God. Ezra Taft Benson is a living prophet. Jesus is the Christ. I bear my humble testimony in the name of Jesus Christ, amen."

Then he returned to his seat. In all my years as a Muslim, I had never seen a child addressing adults on spiritual matters. When the boy first began speaking, I was floored. He spoke plainly. His message was simple, yet powerful. I knew the boy's father, who worked at the Nigerian embassy.

Gaston could see that I was taken by the boy. The Church of Jesus Christ of Latter-day Saints, Gaston told me, encourages children to participate in worship services.

To me that sounded improper. Yet it felt so right. It caused me to question, once again, the aspect of my Muslim upbringing that emphasized the evil nature of Christianity. This boy was humble, meek, and sincere, not exactly qualities associated with evil.

There's something here, I kept telling myself. I felt as if an invisible rope were pulling me. The words people spoke were persuasive. But the feeling they conveyed in those words left a more powerful impression.

Sunday School was another new concept. Latter-day Saints gather in classrooms for an hour to learn more in-depth teachings of Christ. Gaston took me to a class with other individuals who were learning the basics of Latter-day Saint theology. It was not what I expected.

I was used to an imam shouting at his people. But this teacher was leading a discussion, facilitating a conversation. No yelling. No anger.

Very peculiar.

At the conclusion of the services, an older couple approached. They extended their hands and introduced themselves as humanitarian services volunteers from California.

"What is your name?"

"Muhammad Awal."

"Are you a Muslim?"

"Yes. I am a student of Islamic studies at the university."

I'm not really sure why I told them about being a student. The truth was that I was no longer at Al-Azhar. I guess I just wanted them to know who and what they were dealing with.

"Well, we are happy to have you with us today."

"Thank you. I want to visit your church again."

"You are always welcome."

"Do you have anything I can read?"

At my request, the couple handed me a Bible and a Book of Mormon. They were both leather bound. I caressed the covers. Then I felt the tissue-thin pages. I had never held a Bible before. Ever. My father had always forbidden me to look at a Bible.

Although I had discussed some New Testament history with my friend Chuks when I attended the institute in Damascus, that wasn't the same as reading the Bible.

The books felt heavy, in more ways than one. Just handling them, I felt I had crossed a threshold of no return. When I got back to my apartment that afternoon, I immediately started reading Genesis. The names I encountered there were familiar to me: Adam and Eve, Noah and the ark, Abraham and Isaac, Joseph of Egypt, and Moses. They are all mentioned in the Qur'an.

But as I pressed further in the Old Testament, I began to see more and more names and stories that were completely foreign to me. I read all afternoon and into the evening. Friday nights I normally spent drinking at a local pub. But I couldn't put down the Bible. There was something incredibly liberating about being able to experience something that had always been forbidden. I went through that with pop music. But this was different. I knew I was doing something that went against my religious upbringing. Yet I didn't feel guilty. I felt uplifted and informed and enlightened.

I ended up spending the entire weekend working my way through the Old Testament. I didn't leave my apartment once. By the start of the new week I had finished the one thousand-plus page book and turned my attention to the New Testament. I studied the title page:

THE NEW TESTAMENT

OF OUR LORD AND SAVIOUR

JESUS CHRIST

Translated out of the original Greek: and with the former
translations diligently compared and revised,
by his Majesty's special command

It was the King James Version, published by The Church of Jesus Christ of Latter-day Saints in Salt Lake City, Utah, USA.

These particulars intrigued me. Again, I paused to contemplate the fact that I had in my hands a book that Christians throughout the world considered holy writ. It had been commissioned by England's King James and subsequently published by a church in America. Upon my request, members from that church had freely given the book to me.

I ran my hand over its tissue-thin pages before finally turning to the first book in the New Testament, The Gospel According to St Matthew. The headnote of the first chapter said: "Christ is born of Mary—She conceives by the power of the Holy Ghost—Our Lord is named Jesus."

With the enthusiasm of a treasure seeker, I started reading about the birth of Jesus Christ. But I was quickly disappointed to discover that only eight verses were dedicated to this momentous event. It seemed like short shrift for the central figure of Christianity.

Plus, there was almost no mention of Christ's mother, Mary, other than to say that she was a virgin and that the child within her was conceived of the Holy Ghost.

The Qur'an provides much more detail, including dialogue between an angel and the virgin Mary:

"The angel said to Mary: 'Mary, God has chosen you and made you pure: He has truly chosen you above all women. Mary, be devout to your Lord, prostrate yourself in worship, bow down with those who pray.'

"The angel said, 'Mary, God gives you news of a Word from Him, whose name will be the Messiah, Jesus, son of Mary, who will be held in honor in this world and the next, who will be one of those brought near to God. He will speak to people in his infancy and in his adulthood. He will be one of the righteous.'

"She said, 'My Lord, how can I have a son when no man has touched me?'

"The angel said, 'This is how God creates what He will: when He has ordained something, He only says, "Be," and it is.'"

The dialogue in the Qur'an goes on and on between Mary and the angel. I expected to find a similar format in the New Testament, only with even more content. But it wasn't so.

I was amazed that the Qur'an dedicated more pages to Mary than the Bible did.

Then I got to the parables of Jesus. I had warm memories of listening to my father use allegories to teach the principles of Islam. That was one of my father's strong suits—storytelling as a teaching method. It quickly became apparent to me that Christ was a master storyteller. I couldn't help wondering if my father had secretly read the New Testament. The parable of the prodigal son reminded me of my favorite moral story that my father used to tell:

"But when he was yet a great way off, his father saw him, and had compassion, and ran, and fell on his neck, and kissed him.

"And the son said unto him, Father, I have sinned against heaven, and in thy sight, and am no more worthy to be called thy son.

"But the father said to his servants, Bring forth the best robe, and put it on him; and put a ring on his hand, and shoes on his feet:

"And bring hither the fatted calf, and kill it; and let us eat, and be merry:

"For this my son was dead, and is alive again; he was lost, and is found."

My eyes welled up. It felt like yesterday that I had sat at my father's feet and listened to him tell of the African boy who disappeared to England for five years, leaving his parents to conclude that he was dead, before finally returning as the prodigal son. I was so innocent then. But I had become that prodigal son. I was a drunk and a womanizer. I had strayed from everything my father had taught me and embraced many of the vices that he abhorred.

Feeling guilty and miserable, I buried my face in my hands and sobbed. My father would never take me back now. I could hardly blame him. I didn't deserve to be forgiven. I was a sinner. I rubbed my eyes with my fists, as if I could somehow scrub the filth off me. Through all those years of living by such strict rules of obedience, I never experienced what it felt like to feel so unworthy, so hopeless. But now I knew.

Wiping my eyes and nose, I read the parable of the prodigal son again. "Please, God, let this be true," I whispered. "Let this be true."

Then I read the parable of the shepherd who left his ninety-nine sheep to rescue the lost one. "Is that Christianity?" I asked myself. "Going after the lost?"

I got down on my knees. All my mistakes flashed through my mind. I saw Aaban's face when she learned I had slept with Fatima. I saw her tears. I saw the pain I had caused her. I had betrayed the person who loved me the most. I saw myself waking up time and time again in the middle of the day with a hangover. I had dropped out of college. I had no profession. I had no religion. I had been cut off from my family. I was lost in every sense of the word.

Feeling too guilty to pray, I reached for my New Testament. Reading, I hoped, would bring some solace. Still kneeling, I turned to the page containing the account of the adulteress who was caught in the act and taken before Jesus to be stoned. My mind drifted back twenty years or more to a time when I was six or seven. I was out in front of my house with a bunch of boys from my neighborhood when a Christian girl passed by on the main road heading into town. We knew she was Christian because she had on pants and a sleeveless shirt. Muslim girls weren't allowed to dress that way.

"A monkey in trousers," one of my friends shouted.

The girl could not have been more than seventeen. She just looked straight ahead and kept walking.

"Monkey in trousers," another boy shouted.

She picked up her pace.

A couple of boys picked up stones and threw them at her. She started running. More boys picked up bigger rocks and gave chase. The rocks struck her back and knocked her to the ground. A group of men outside the mosque witnessed the scene but did nothing to stop it. As the boys descended on her, a man emerged from a car and grabbed the girl. Blood trickled down her face. Her bare arms were bloody, too. The man placed her in the backseat. As he drove off, the boys hurled rocks at his car, shattering the back window.

I didn't throw rocks that day. But I ran with the boys who did. It was just so easy to go along with the mob.

I returned to the account of the adulteress in the New Testament. I could visualize the religious leaders—these men in their robes—standing over this woman, clamoring for Jesus to uphold the law, which called for the woman to be stoned to death. It was Christ's response that I couldn't picture. He's drawing in the dirt with his finger when he looks up and says let him who is without sin cast the first stone. And one by one, the religious leaders turn and depart. Alone with the woman, Christ encourages her to sin no more. But he doesn't punish her.

My eyes welled up again. "I want to be judged like that," I cried. "I want another chance to sin no more."

For the next few weeks, I attended services with the Mormon congregation. During that time I completely avoided alcohol and cigarettes. Being around those people made me want to live as they did. I also spent every spare minute reading. I loved reading the four Gospels in the New Testament.

The Gospel of John made a pretty compelling case for Jesus being the Only Begotten Son of God. Muslims don't agree. Sura number 112 in the Qur'an says that God begot no one. There is no divine Son of God. Case closed.

But I couldn't resist the feeling that Christ was the Son of God. I wasn't just taking this on faith, because at that point I didn't have much faith. But the concept of a divine Christ actually made sense to me on an intellectual level. The fact that he was willing to lay down his own life to redeem his people had convinced me that this was the hallmark of a true Savior.

Muslims believe salvation comes through sacrifice. The New Testament says that Christ made the ultimate sacrifice for all mankind. I thought about Peter lopping off the ear of the soldier who tried to seize Jesus in the Garden of Gethsemane. Jesus, according to the Bible, immediately healed his captor by restoring his ear. The God of Islam would never act that way. But Jesus wasn't finished. He then surrendered to the soldiers and went to prison, knowing that he would be crucified. That's the part that most Muslims, at least the ones I grew up with, cannot associate with divinity. Gods, or divine beings, are not supposed to submit to man. It's supposed to be the other way around.

Warm tears streamed down my cheeks as I imagined the scene of Christ submitting to evil men in order to save his people from their sins. I longed to be one of his people. I ached for redemption.

When I finished the New Testament, I turned to the Book of Mormon. I assumed it would be just like the Bible, but it wasn't.

First I learned that Mormon was an ancient prophet, much like Moses and Abraham. Second, his name is on the book because he was the one who took what amounted to 1,000 years' worth of writings from other ancient prophets and condensed them into a single volume. The central theme of the Book of Mormon is that Jesus Christ is the Savior of the world and that after his resurrection he appeared in the ancient Americas.

Members of The Church of Jesus Christ of Latter-day Saints believe that in 1823 in upstate New York an angel appeared to a boy prophet named Joseph Smith and directed him to a location where Mormon's writing had been deposited in the ground. With the help of numerous scribes, Smith translated the records into English and published the first edition of the Book of Mormon in Palmyra, New York, in 1830.

The scenario overwhelmed me. The part about an angel appearing to a prophet wasn't hard to accept. Muslims believe in such occurrences. What intrigued me the most was the account of Jesus

Christ spreading his gospel to a region of the world far removed from the Middle East. The later part of the Book of Mormon described Christ descending out of heaven and saying:

"Behold, I am Jesus Christ, whom the prophets testified shall come into the world.

"And behold, I am the light and life of the world; and I have drunk out of that bitter cup which the Father hath given me, and have glorified the Father in taking upon me the sins of the world, in the which I have suffered the will of the Father in all things from the beginning."

The people had fallen to the ground in amazement. Christ admonished them to stand up: "Arise and come forth unto me, that ye may thrust your hands into my side, and also that ye may feel the prints of the nails in my hands and in my feet, that ye may know that I am the God of Israel, and the God of the whole earth, and have been slain for the sins of the world."

Those words—"the God of the whole earth"—really threw me. That went counter to everything I had been taught as a Muslim. Islam doesn't treat Jesus as divine. The Qur'an specifically says that "those who say, 'God is the Messiah, the son of Mary' are defying the truth." As evidence for this, the Qur'an points out that if Christ were truly the Messiah, God would not have allowed him to be destroyed.

That kind of logic had always made sense to me. Suddenly it didn't. The Book of Mormon presented a more compelling scenario, one in which a divine being chose to lay down his life in order to save his people. Christ died for man's sins. Moreover, his resurrection paved the way for mankind to overcome death.

"But is this true?" I asked myself. "Did Christ really make an appearance in the ancient Americas?"

It made sense to me that Christ would choose to visit people besides the Jews. Then I remembered reading in the New Testament that Jesus said he was going to visit his other sheep. The Book of

Mormon claims to be a record of Christ's other sheep, those who left Jerusalem six hundred years before his birth.

I used some of the logic I had learned as a Muslim to work my way through the situation. If one believes that Jesus ascended to the heavens, then one has to believe he has the power to appear anywhere. And if one can believe that he rose from the dead, one certainly must accept the possibility that he is capable of appearing somewhere else on the planet. What is harder to believe, that he rose from the dead or that he appeared on more than one continent?

Then I broke it down even more simply. If Jesus Christ is divine, he can appear to people in another part of the world. If one doesn't believe he can do this, one belittles him.

I concluded he had visited the people in America. Tears filled my eyes as I visualized them touching the nail marks in Christ's palms. I wanted to touch those nail marks myself. For the first time in my life I wanted to be in Christ's presence. I never thought I'd feel something like that. But the words of the Bible and the Book of Mormon had stirred my soul. It's hard to describe what I felt. But it was unlike anything I had ever encountered while reading the Qur'an or any other book.

I had always believed that Jesus is not divine. Now I believed that he is.

CHAPTER 19

BETRAYAL

Consumed with learning as much as I could about Christianity, I had been seeing less of Aaban. One evening I returned to my apartment and found her inside, waiting for me. She was holding my Bible and had tears in her eyes.

"Did one of your friends bring you this book?" she demanded.

I took offense at her tone. "No," I told her. "Those are my books. Don't you see my name on them?"

"What are you doing with these books?"

"What are books for?" I asked rhetorically. "They are to read."

"But you cannot do this thing," she insisted.

"What do you mean I can't do this? Listen, if I don't read this, how do I know if my own religion is the right one or the wrong one?"

That didn't register with Aaban.

"I'm finding so many answers," I continued. "I invite you to read it."

"What!"

After that exchange we didn't speak for about a week. Then one afternoon she told me that she had received a call from the leader of the Northern Nigerian Student Union at Al-Azhar. This puzzled me. I had cut off contact with those guys nearly a year earlier. The last time I had talked with any of them was before my run-in with my professor and the car accident a few days later.

"What could they possibly want with me now?" I asked her.

"They said it was urgent," she said. "They need to see you."

That evening I paid them a visit. Most of them lived together in a big house that was owned by a sheik from Nigeria. The sons of a few prominent Nigerian politicians lived in the house. When I arrived, the guys who wanted to see me were crowded into a living room area. Most of them were sitting on chairs that lined the walls, making the space feel very cramped.

"My girlfriend said you wanted to talk to me," I said coldly.

"Sit down," one of them said. Then he turned to one of the others. "Bring Awal some tea."

"I don't drink tea anymore," I said.

This drew strange expressions.

"Would you like some coffee instead?"

"No, thank you."

"Juice?" one of them asked.

"Sure."

After about fifteen minutes of small talk, other leaders of the Northern Nigerian Student Union showed up. They wore grave expressions. I immediately assumed something tragic had happened back home, perhaps a death in the family.

"What has happened?" I asked.

"We learned that you have Christian books in your home," one of the leaders said.

I was stunned. That was the last thing I expected them to say. Maybe I heard them wrong. Maybe this was just a bad dream.

"What?" I said.

"You heard what I said," the man repeated. "Don't pretend."

"Yes, I have," I snapped. "Is there a problem with that?"

"You have to get rid of them."

"Why?"

"Because it's no good reading them."

"Why? In school they want us to preach to Christians and pagans. If you don't read their books, how can you talk to them?"

"What do you mean?"

"Islamic critics say this and that, but they don't read their books. We need to read their books to know what is in their mind."

One of the leaders of the group rose to his feet. "This boy has gone too far," he said. "The devil is stuck in him."

"He dresses like modern Egyptians," another one said. "He listens to Western music. Smokes cigarettes. We are ordering you to get rid of those books."

"Look, I'm just reading, and I don't think there is any harm in reading."

I stood to leave.

One of them stood and blocked my path. "Sit down!"

"I am going," I said.

"We are talking to you," he shouted. "The devil has sway on you. Just look at the way you are dressed."

Another guy grabbed the one in my path and pulled him back. "Calm down," he told his friend. "Relax."

The leader of the group finally stood. "If you can't throw those books away, then at least return them to their owner. And tell him you don't want to read them anymore."

"You are a brother," another one of them chimed in. "You are one of us. We don't want you to go astray."

"When we go home, we will be asked why we didn't force you to stop reading," the leader said. "We could have beaten you. But we don't want to do that. We like you. You are one of us. But you can't play with this thing."

"Let's pray and close this meeting," another one of them suggested.

All eyes were on me. "Okay," I said.

Everybody raised their hands in the air. "In the name of Allah," one of them began, "it is you we worship. It is you we ask for help. Guide us to the straight path, the path of those you have blessed, those who incur no anger and who have not gone astray.

"Allah, our brother Awal has gone astray. The devil is leading him.

"Allah, lead Awal to the right path.

"Allah, turn the evil ones away from our brother Awal that he may continue to be righteous. Amen."

"Amen!" the group said in response.

On the commute back across town to my apartment, I couldn't shake the sense of fear I felt. At the same time, I couldn't get over the fact that members of the Northern Nigerian Student Union knew what I was reading. That mystified me. After all, I kept those books hidden in my apartment. As far as I knew, those guys didn't know my address. So how did they know what I was reading?

Then it dawned on me. Aaban. She was the only one who had been in my apartment since I acquired the Bible and the Book of Mormon. She was also the one who had insisted that I go see the head of the Northern Nigerian Student Union. She had exposed me.

My stomach got queasy. My legs got weak. As soon as I reached the apartment I shared with Dutch, I lay down on the couch. I hadn't been there long when the doorbell rang. I opened it and found Aaban standing there. She kissed both of my cheeks and then followed me to my bedroom, where she sat down on the edge of the bed.

"Tell me," I said. "When did you see the guys from Al-Azhar?"

"Why?"

"You know why I'm asking. When did you see them?"

"My love, I have tried to talk to you. You don't listen to me. Somebody has to talk to you."

"You have betrayed me."

She said nothing.

"You have betrayed my trust."

She still said nothing.

"If you were going to talk to them, you might as well have just gone straight to my father. I never thought you would do this." I shook my head. "This is like giving them a knife to stab me. I don't think I'll ever forgive you."

She started sobbing.

I walked out of my bedroom. I was so angry I didn't want to look at her.

Pacing back and forth in the living room, I waited for her to leave. But she didn't come out of my room.

"I'm sorry," she cried when I reentered the bedroom.

"I have never felt betrayed by you," I told her. "Never."

"I'm so sorry."

"If you had caught me with a girl and you went and talked to her, I wouldn't mind that. But this is my personal issue. What I read is my business."

"You are not thinking of us or our love," she said. "You are only thinking of your own selfish interests."

"You are starting again. One minute you say you're sorry. Another minute you are criticizing me."

She started crying again. "If you had listened to me and gotten rid of those books, all of this would have been avoided."

I stormed back out of my bedroom. Dutch was in the living room working on a story. "Hey, what's happening?" he said.

"Nothing," I said.

I sat down on the couch and waited for Aaban to leave my room.

"Are you going out with me tonight?" Dutch said.

"I don't know," I said. I could feel my anger mounting. I went back in my bedroom. She was still on my bed. We just stared at each other in silence.

"I never knew you could do something like this to me," I said.

"I was only looking out for your welfare," she said.

"So you go and tell *them*? And you ask me to go there without telling me anything?"

"I'm sorry."

"I can't trust you anymore."

She was scared.

I was wounded.

Both of us sensed that a seismic change had just occurred in our relationship.

"Wait," she pleaded.

"No. It's over!"

We both stared at each other.

Was this really happening?

It was. We were unraveling. She pleaded with me to come to my senses, to not overreact.

But she had already overreacted when she went behind my back and notified the Muslim students from Nigeria that I was reading the Bible. That was like a knife in the back. They'd be out to destroy me now. My father would find out. People would come after me.

She tried to argue that the whole problem would disappear if I'd simply get rid of the Bible and any other Christian books.

There was no way I was doing that. Besides, it wasn't that simple. The damage had been done. In the eyes of the members of the Nigerian Muslims at Al-Azhar, I had already defected.

Aaban still wanted me to abandon any association with Christianity. She told me I had a choice to make. It was either her or the books.

I didn't need time to think. "I choose my books," I said softly.

She stared at me blankly.

"I choose my books," I repeated.

Crying, Aaban fled my apartment.

Dutch knew how much I cared for Aaban. He also knew that I had been delving into Christianity. He entered my bedroom and found me crying. "I'm headed to the English pub around the corner," he said. "Why don't you come with me?"

I just sat there.

"C'mon," he said. "It will do you good to get out."

I got up and followed him out.

On the way, he said to me, "What's going on between you and Aaban?"

"She's mad at me."

"Why?"

"Because I'm reading the Bible and going to a Christian church."

"I see."

By the time we reached the pub, I was a mess. My anger had turned to sadness. "I loved her," I told Dutch. "It's over."

He could see that I was crying.

"I miss her already," I said.

"She'll be back," he said.

"No. She won't. We're through. It's over."

The bartender approached. "What'll you have?"

"One beer and one orange juice," Dutch said.

More than ever I wanted a drink. But Dutch wouldn't let me. We stayed at the pub for an hour. He kept telling me that things would get better.

Less than twenty-four hours after breaking off things with Aaban, I received an unexpected visit at my apartment. A couple of members of the Northern Nigerian Student Union showed up. I kept the chain on the door and opened it just wide enough to see them through the crack. I asked what they wanted. They said they had come to give me an ultimatum: Destroy the Christian books or be destroyed.

"You cannot give me orders," I said. "Now leave."

They were so arrogant that my defiance shocked them. I should have been too frightened to stand up to them. But I was coming apart. Maybe it was the fact that I had lost Aaban. Or maybe I was tired of being bullied by Islam. It could have been a combination of the two. In any event, I unchained my door and took a step toward the men. "I said leave," I repeated, glaring at them.

We were inches from violence. My hands were shaking.

Scowling, the men slowly nodded their heads up and down, as if to say—let the battle begin. Without saying a word, they turned and walked off.

I went back inside and collapsed on the couch. I knew I was in trouble.

The next day my father called from Nigeria. He didn't bother to say hello.

"What is this that we hear?" he boomed. "You have moved in with a Jew!"

I didn't bother telling him that Dutch wasn't Jewish.

"It's not enough that you disgraced me in Syria," he continued. "Now you are carrying Bibles around?"

I said nothing.

"You have gone too far," he said. "This is why I didn't want you to go to Cairo from the beginning. You have gone astray," he continued. "I disown you. I wish you never carried my name."

He screamed at me.

I cried.

He didn't say good-bye.

Neither did I.

CHAPTER 20

BORN AGAIN

More than eighty million people reside in Egypt. Approximately 90 percent of them are Sunni Muslims. Most of the remaining 10 percent are known as Coptic Christians, a term that refers broadly to Egypt's community of Christians. Although most Christians in Egypt consider themselves Copts, not all do. Mormons are among the 1 percent that doesn't.

Despite being a distinct minority, Coptic Christians are afforded equal protection under Egyptian law. In other words, they are free to practice their religion. But reports of discrimination and abuse by Islamic fundamentalists against Copts are not uncommon. Still, at least Copts enjoy protection on paper. Mormons don't have even that. Today, Egypt does not recognize The Church of Jesus Christ of Latter-day Saints. It is illegal for Mormons to proselytize. Any attempt to convert Muslims is strictly forbidden by the church.

I represented a very unusual case. The church didn't seek me out. I pursued the church. My curiosity had led me to ask questions. The answers I found inspired me to a belief in Mormonism. Yet I faced a dilemma. Leaving Islam and becoming a Mormon would make me a marked man. I would be judged a heathen and an infidel. It wouldn't be safe for me to set foot in Nigeria, at least not any-where near my home. My father had already disowned me. But re-ceiving baptism would be interpreted as an act of blasphemy against Allah.

But I had no choice, I told myself. I had compiled quite a col-lection of sins. More than anything, I wanted a clean conscience. I told the Mormon leaders in Cairo that I wanted to be baptized.

To my surprise, they told me no. The church simply did not have the legal authority to baptize Muslims in Egypt, and Mormon policy prohibited it. I could attend church and act like a Mormon. I just couldn't be one.

Baptism or no baptism, I figured no one could stop me from accepting Christ as my Savior and living my life as a Christian. So I decided to make some big changes. First, I quit my job as a DJ and found a full-time job as a translator. If I was going to become a Christian, I figured I had to get away from the club scene. I was for-tunate to hire on with an agency that provided Arabic translation to English-speaking professionals in Cairo. Next, I decided I didn't want to be called Muhammad anymore. I wanted a Christian name instead. I chose Tito, the Italian version of Titus, which was the name of a missionary companion to the Apostle Paul. The more I learned about Titus, the more I felt a connection to him. Christians initially rejected Titus for not being circumcised. The situation be-came a bit of a test case for Paul, who went to Jerusalem and argued that circumcision shouldn't be forced on Titus.

Titus was an outsider. I was too. At least I felt like one when I attended Mormon church meetings in Cairo. The people made me feel welcome, but I couldn't be baptized. And without baptism, I didn't feel completely accepted.

For months I kept asking to be baptized, but I was told the same thing every time: Wait. During that time, members of the congregation were praying that my wish would come true. I was praying too.

Eventually, I was told that a way had been found for me to be baptized. I finally had my wish. Arrangements were made for me to travel to a location where the baptism could be performed.

A member gave me some advice.

"Tito, baptism by immersion has symbolic significance," he told me. "It is important to be fully immersed in water. You bury everything down there. As you rise out of that water, that's the new birth."

"Yes."

He looked me in the eye. "Before you take this step, I want to be sure you realize that there is no going back after baptism."

I nodded.

"You are going into deep water, Tito."

I knew he didn't mean that literally. He was referring to a depth of commitment.

He looked me in the eye. "You understand what you are about to do?" he asked.

I stared into his eyes, remembering the words of Christ to his disciples: "Whosoever shall seek to save his life shall lose it; and whosoever shall lose his life shall preserve it." All of a sudden I felt scared.

But I nodded affirmatively. This was no time, I told myself, to look back.

He embraced me. "You are ready, Tito."

A few members of the Church were able to attend the baptism. I changed out of my street clothes into white baptismal clothes. Standing barefoot, I looked in the mirror, tears streaming down my cheeks. I was overjoyed and frightened, a weird combination of emotions. I kept reminding myself that Latter-day Saints believe in life after death. They also believe that the gift of resurrection is not exclusive to Christians. Everyone is resurrected. All I could do was hope that when my parents reached the other side, they'd recognize that salvation comes through Jesus Christ. Maybe then they would thank me for having the courage to accept Christ during my lifetime.

CHAPTER 21

DEEP WATER

I felt like a new man. I was sober. I had a job as a translator. Best of all, I could look at myself in the mirror.

But I also had to keep looking over my shoulder. The students from the Northern Nigerian Student Union at Al-Azhar were furious with me, and my family was too. Of course it wasn't safe for me to return to Nigeria. But I didn't feel safe in Cairo, either. What I needed was a new identity and a new home, a place where the people who despised me couldn't find me.

One day the phone rang, and I answered it.

"Peace be unto you," said the voice on the other end.

The Nigerian telephone greeting. The voice was vaguely familiar, but I couldn't place it.

"Is this Muhammad Awal?" the man asked.

"Yes."

"Are you alone?"

"Yes."

"Are you sure?"

"Yes."

"I don't want anyone to know that I spoke with you. Can you promise that?"

"With whom am I speaking?" I said.

"You will know. Just assure me that no one will know that I called you."

"Yes. Yes. Just tell me who you are."

He told me his name. I took a deep breath. It was one of my cousins. "You scared me," I told him.

"You should be scared," he said.

"Why?"

"Stop asking questions and just listen to me."

"Okay."

"May the remaining years be added to your own," he began.

"Oh, my God!" In the Arab world, those words signal that someone has died. "Who is it?"

"It is Eve."

"What?" I sank into the sofa.

"Your mother," he said.

"What happened?"

"That's why I'm calling. Please don't let anybody know—"

"Just tell me!"

"It was suicide."

I dropped the phone. It hurt to breathe.

"Whatever they tell you," I could hear him saying, "isn't true. It was suicide. She got pushed so far that she couldn't take the pressure anymore."

Shaking, I fumbled for the phone. "Cousin," I cried.

"Muhammad," he said, "your father is in a rage. The elders are in a rage. Your stepbrothers are in a rage. They were all accusing her

189

of being at fault for your being an infidel. They couldn't get at you, so they took it out on her. They were ruthless."

"Oh, God, no! No."

"You have to listen to me, Muhammad," he said. "They may try and trick you into going back to Nigeria by telling you she got very ill and died. But don't believe them. Don't ever come back. They will kill you if you come back here."

He hung up.

I dropped to my knees and pounded the couch with my fist. For the first time in my life, I hated Aaban. Hated her! I had told her that her decision to go to the Brotherhood on campus would lead to no good. "If she were here right now I would kill her," I swore.

Weeping, I went to my room and dug out the photographs I had taken of my mother. I put the pictures to my chest. I felt so alone. I felt hideously guilty, too. My mother was the sweetest human being I knew. She had the patience of Job. She put up with my father. She put up with orthodoxy and male dominance. She raised six children. Her life was plain hard. But it turned out that the hardest thing she ever had to do was be my mother.

Baptism suddenly felt like the biggest mistake of my life. It was more than a mistake. It was foolish and reckless and had resulted in tragedy. If I had not converted to Christianity, my mother would be alive. It was that simple.

I started to question my own purpose for living.

Then I remembered what I had felt moments before I got baptized.

This is going to change my life.

There is no turning back.

I just need to go into the water. I need to go deep.

Losing my mother was deeper water than I had imagined.

CHAPTER 22

NOWHERE
TO HIDE

I'm not sure why, but I got up and went to church the next day. That simple decision may have saved me from going off the deep end. When I was in the company of other Christians, I was reminded what Christ suffered. I asked myself: *Is this what it means to be a true Christian?*

For the next couple of weeks I felt lost. My sadness turned to fury. I wanted revenge. I wanted to lash out. Then one day I was walking through a hotel lobby in Cairo—I don't even remember why I was there—and I bumped into Aaban. It had been months since we last spoke. The moment I spotted her, I could feel the rage escalating in me. She was with a guy. As she and I passed by each other, we were close enough that our arms nearly brushed. She saw me but said nothing. That was a good thing. I'm afraid I would have become violent if she had opened her mouth.

That was the last time I ever saw her.

Within three weeks of my mother's suicide, Dutch tracked me down at a friend's house. He said he was calling me from a pay phone. "The police were just at my place asking for you," he said. "They were in plain clothes. But they were very aggressive."

Normally, Dutch didn't get excited about the Egyptian authorities. For instance, he had known for a long time that his phone was tapped. But he shrugged that off, saying that all the foreign journalists assumed their phones were tapped. No big deal. Such is life in the Middle East.

But I could tell from his voice that he was worried about the police showing up at his apartment. There was only one reason the police would want to see me. The members of the Northern Nigerian Student Union at Al-Azhar had to have reported me. And I had no doubt that my father and my stepbrothers had put them up to it. The police and security force in Cairo were notoriously corrupt. They were also predominantly Muslim. That combination worked against me as a Christian convert. I was convinced that the officers had been influenced to do anything necessary to take me into custody.

"I don't think you should come back to my place," Dutch said. "The authorities will be back."

"Okay."

"Do you have a place where you can stay for a couple of weeks?"

"I have a friend I can stay with."

"I will meet you at the metro station in a few hours. Tell me what you need me to bring you."

That night, Dutch entered the metro station near his apartment wearing a baseball cap, a white T-shirt, and jeans. He handed me a duffel bag full of my things. "You need to find a way out of Egypt," he said. "It's time for you to go."

"I know."

"Do you have any money on you?" he asked.

"Yes."

"How much?"

"About $100."

"That's not enough."

He reached into his pocket and pulled out a wad of cash. "Here," he said. "This should hold you over for a little while."

I shoved the money into my pocket.

"How can I get hold of you?" he asked.

I gave him the number where I'd be staying.

I thought about going to the church for help. There were plenty of people there who had the means and the know-how to assist me. But I was afraid of dragging them into the mess I was in. Even Dutch thought I'd be putting church members at risk by going to them for help. Given the situation, the best thing I could do was stay away from the church altogether. The last thing I wanted was for Egyptian authorities to show up at church services looking for me. That could lead to church members being treated as guilty by association.

What I needed was an alias and a passport. There was a good chance that my name was on a watch-list, so getting out of the country was going to be risky and expensive. I reached out to a friend from Chad. He was a Muslim and his family resided in a neighborhood in Cairo that was almost exclusively occupied by Chadians. I had known the family since my days at Al-Azhar, and they had allowed me to sleep and eat at their home during various periods of hardship since my decision to become a Christian. Despite my decision to leave Islam, they still treated me like family.

As soon as I told my Chadian friend about my situation, he spoke to a contact of his at the Chadian Embassy. The embassy contact was capable of helping me obtain an alias and a passport for travel to Canada through Spain. The cost would be about $4,000. My friend's family said they'd cover the costs.

But it was going to take about two weeks to pull everything together. In the meantime, my friend advised me to stay put in the

Chadian neighborhood. The police would never look for me there. I slept on his living room floor and stopped going to my translating job. I stopped going just about everywhere.

Everything I was planning was illegal: lying about my identity, forging documents, misleading customs officials. But I was dealing with a corrupt system. If I played by their rules, I'd end up in custody anyway. Better to go underground and sneak out of Egypt before it was too late.

The wisdom in this approach was confirmed while I was waiting for my new name and passport to come through. One evening I went for a walk in my friend's neighborhood. While passing a coffee shop, I made eye contact with a man inside. He was seated at a window table, and I immediately recognized him from the nightclub where I used to be a DJ. He had a thick mustache and a penchant for downing lots of whiskey.

I had always maintained a very friendly relationship with him at the club. But it scared me to see him now. I knew he worked for the Egyptian state security. I couldn't imagine what he was doing at some coffee shop in a Chadian neighborhood far away from the center of Cairo.

Was he onto me?

With his fat index finger, he motioned for me to step inside.

I wanted to run. But something told me not to. I ducked in and pulled up a chair.

"Will I see you at the disco soon?" he asked.

"Yes," I told him. I planned to be back at the club soon. I lied. I figured he'd get suspicious if I told him otherwise.

"You better not," he said firmly.

Clearly I had misread him. Trying to maintain a stoic expression, I asked him what he meant.

"They are after you," he whispered. "You better get out of Egypt."

I nodded my head as a chill ran down my spine.

"You never tell anybody that you saw me," he continued.

I nodded again.

Then he turned away from me as if I was a stranger.

Grateful, I headed for the door without saying good-bye. In Egypt, a tip like that is worth gold.

Later that night, I told my Chadian friend about the encounter. He said not to worry. Things were progressing on his end. Soon, he assured me, I'd have a new name, a new birth date, and a new place of birth, along with round-trip airfare to Canada through Madrid. Under the new paperwork I'd be listed as a Chadian, which would enable me to get through customs at the airport in Cairo without detection. But once I changed planes in Spain, I was told I'd need to destroy my passport and other documentation before landing in Canada. Then when I appeared before Canadian customs officials, I should surrender to the Canadian authorities and claim that I was from Somalia, Ethiopia, or Liberia. All three were in the midst of war, and individuals from those countries were granted asylum in Canada.

It didn't make complete sense to me. And the whole plan was inherently risky. But there was no other plan. And my liberty was at stake. I was willing to try anything.

CHAPTER 23

THY WILL
BE DONE

It was early in the morning when my Chadian friend burst through the door of his home with airline tickets and my new passport. The name on both said Adam Islam. That was my new name. Not very original. But I was grateful and anxious. My flight was due to leave in a few hours. That meant I had very little time to get to the airport and memorize my new birthday, place of birth, home address, and other vital information.

My years of training memorizing the Qur'an came in handy. By the time we got to the Cairo airport, I had everything down. The trick was going to be acting relaxed if a customs official asked me to recite any of this information.

Thy will be done. I kept telling myself that as I made my way past the check-in counter and then onto customs. The agent's eyes went from me to my passport and back again. Then he scrutinized my paperwork. It was the longest sixty seconds of my life. Finally, he handed me my passport and let me pass. Next I went through a simple pat-down search.

By the time I approached the gate my shirt was soaked with sweat. I felt as if I had just run a marathon. I was completely drained. I practically collapsed when I boarded the plane and found my seat. The roar of the jet engine might as well have been a choir of angels from heaven. Once we started to taxi down the runway, I finally felt safe.

I kept thanking God as we became airborne. I cried as I looked down on the pyramids, the River Nile, and all the familiar places I had come to know so well. "Good-bye," I whispered, my face pressed against the window.

I had fallen in love with Cairo. The first time I went through there as a sixteen-year-old en route to Syria, the city had seemed wicked to me. That was then. Living there had changed me. It was the place where I had found my first love. It was where I discovered Western culture. It was big, fast, and diverse . . . and so far away from Nigeria. Maybe it was the atmosphere. But I had felt safe there, safe enough to let down my guard and experiment with such new things as music, alcohol, and professional pursuits outside the clergy. Some of those things brought me heartache and pain. But without them I never would have found the gospel of Jesus Christ. That, more than anything, had changed my life and opened my eyes to possibilities that had been impossible to imagine as a young man being trained for the clergy in Islam.

Strangely, I had come full circle with Cairo. As the city faded out of view, I saw it as evil again. Not the people or the culture, but the political regime, particularly the police, was so corrupt that someone in my shoes had to live in fear. Not anymore. I put my head back and fell asleep.

By the time I woke up, the plane was descending. I had never been in Spain before. And though I was scheduled to spend only a few hours in the airport, I was eager to have a look around.

When I stepped off the plane, a couple of security officers were positioned just inside the terminal. One of them motioned me toward him with his hand. "Passport," he said.

I handed it to him.

He flipped through it. Then he looked at me. Then said something in Spanish to his colleague.

"Come with me," he said.

I followed him to an immigration counter. A customs official thumbed through my passport and escorted me through the checkpoint and into an office waiting area. "Have a seat," he told me.

I couldn't help being nervous. What if there was something wrong with my paperwork?

Soon an Arab family was escorted in and told to wait. Then a Nigerian man was ushered in. Within minutes, they were cleared and on their way. An hour later, I was still sitting there. Finally, I approached the window. "My flight is leaving in forty-five minutes," I told a man in a uniform.

"They know. They know. Just sit down and wait."

Another fifteen minutes passed, and a uniformed woman entered the waiting area. "Excuse me," I said to her. "I've been waiting here a long time, and I don't know why I'm here. I'm about to miss my connecting flight. Can you help me?"

"I will check for you."

She went behind the glass. I could see her huddling with male officers, one of whom opened a secured door and motioned me toward him with his hand. He had my passport and a boarding pass. "Come with me," he said.

I followed him all the way to baggage claim. "Do you see your bag?" he asked.

I spotted my suitcase against a wall. The officer checked the name tag on the suitcase against my ticket. Then he walked my suitcase and me to customs. After an agent searched my suitcase, the officer led me to the ticket counter for Egypt Air. A ticket agent handed the officer a new ticket for me. I wasn't sure if my flight to Canada had been delayed or if I was being put on a later flight. But as soon as we left the Egypt Air counter, the officer hurriedly led me through the terminal and directly to a gate where flight attendants were waiting. All the other passengers on the flight had already boarded. The officer handed me my passport and rushed me onto the plane. He escorted me all the way to my seat and even helped me get my suitcase on board.

The cabin was hot and packed. But I didn't care. I was just relieved to be on board. The officer rushed off the plane without saying another word, and the next thing I knew the plane was taxiing down the runway. That's when I heard the pilot's voice for the first time.

He was speaking Arabic.

"My God," I said under my breath.

I looked around me. Then I looked over my shoulder. Everyone on board was an Arab. I wasn't heading to Canada. I was on a flight back to Cairo. A feeling of doom swept over me.

Convinced that Egyptian authorities were onto me, I had no doubt they'd be waiting for me when I stepped off the plane in Cairo. I would be arrested. The fake passport in my hand was my ticket to jail. I knew what police custody was like in Egypt. A guy like me—an African Muslim who had converted to Christianity and tried leaving the country with false papers—would be subject to persecution.

I had to do something. But what? I was airborne. There was no place to run. Nowhere to hide. Sitting there, I wished for something I never imagined I'd want. I wished for Palestinian terrorists to hijack the plane and reroute it to Cypress or anyplace besides Cairo. I was that desperate.

Then I had an idea. I unbuckled my seat belt and headed to the restroom. Once inside, I locked the door and tore my passport into tiny pieces. I tore up my ticket, too. Then I flushed them down the toilet. I figured I should at least destroy any evidence that I had falsified my identity. I realized that this created a new problem for me. I was going to have to explain how I got on board with no identification. But I'd cross that bridge when I came to it.

Shortly after I returned to my seat the plane started shaking violently. The turbulence got so bad that it felt like the plane was going to come apart. Cries of "God is great" in Arabic rang throughout the cabin. The cries continued until the plane stabilized just before landing in Cairo. The moment the passengers exited the plane they dropped to their knees on the runway and put their foreheads to the ground, shouting: "God is great. God is great."

I didn't thank God. I wasn't happy to be in Cairo.

Egyptian police officers were waiting for me.

"Welcome back," one of them said to me. "You think you can run away from us?"

I said nothing.

"This is the Salman Rushdie of Egypt," another officer said, triggering laughter amongst his fellow officers.

"Passport," the lead officer said, grinning.

"What passport?" I said.

"Your passport."

"I don't have a passport."

The officer turned out my pockets and went through my carry-on bag. "Where is it?"

"It is with the police in Spain. They kept it when they put me on the plane."

"You are a con man," he said.

"He's the Salman Rushdie of Egypt," one of the lieutenants said.

Everyone laughed.

I didn't think it was funny. Rushdie's 1988 novel *The Satanic Verses* had aroused violent opposition throughout the Muslim world. Many Muslims felt the book was blasphemous toward Muhammad. More than ten countries with a large Muslim population banned the book. In countries where the book was sold, bookstores were bombed and protest rallies were held. Ayatollah Ruhollah Khomeini, the spiritual leader of Iran, called for Rushdie's execution, a move that ultimately led the United Kingdom to break off diplomatic relations with Iran. In the Arab world, there weren't many insults greater than being compared to Salman Rushdie.

I was taken to an interrogation room where an officer was seated at a beat-up wooden table. He had a few more stripes on his uniform and an imposing firearm on his belt. He stood up as a couple of agents pushed me forward. Then one of them grabbed me by the back of the neck and slammed my face down on the wooden table. The corner of my eye caught the corner of the table. Blood immediately started trickling from a gash just above my eyebrow.

"Have a seat," the man behind the desk said. "I don't want to see your contaminated blood on my desk."

Then he turned to one of his deputies. "Clean up his face," he ordered. "And bring him some water."

One of the men wadded up some tissue and patted above my eye. The other guy returned with a glass of water. It tasted foul. But I didn't care. My mouth felt as if I had been chewing on cotton balls.

"Now," the official said, "are you going to cooperate with us or not?"

"Sir, I am cooperating with you."

"Who helped you?"

"Helped me do what?"

"Who helped you leave this country?"

I insisted that I didn't know what he was talking about.

"Look," he told me, "we don't want you. We want those people who helped you. Was it the Americans?"

"I don't have any American friends."

He sprang from his chair and shouted for the guards. Four uniformed men hustled in. They dragged me to a cell. It was dark, dank, and utterly empty. Not even a cot. The guards shoved me inside and secured the lock without saying a word. I didn't see anyone else for the remainder of the day. I was given no food or water. That night I curled up on the concrete floor. I couldn't help questioning God. I asked the same question I had uttered on the plane—why me?

Then I got to my knees and uttered a four-word prayer: "Thy will be done."

Then I lay back down and repeated those same words over and over. No one was around to hear me. But I believed God could hear me. And that was enough.

CHAPTER 24

BEHIND THE SUN

I had a pretty good sense of what I was in for when I woke up stiff and tired. I didn't know the time. I wasn't even sure if it was morning or night. The cell looked the same all the time: dark.

Two guards eventually showed up. They clamped leg irons around my ankles and handcuffs on my wrists. Then they escorted me out of the cell and took me to a room where a fierce-looking official was waiting. He resembled the man who had interrogated me the previous day. Only this guy grinned when I entered the room. It was an evil grin.

"You are in real trouble," he said.

I said nothing, and the guards took their places a few feet behind me.

The official made a final attempt to get me to reveal who had helped me obtain a fake passport. I played dumb.

The official kept grinning. "We will send you behind the sun," he said.

In Arabic, *behind the sun* means "a place of no return."

My interrogator could see that I wasn't going to talk. He motioned for the guards to take me out. They led me to a docking area where a military truck was parked. Other prisoners were in the back.

"Get in," one of the guards said.

The truck delivered us to a state security facility, an intimidating place near the American University in Cairo. I had heard horror stories about what happened to people who were taken there.

I was still in leg irons and handcuffs when security officials pulled me out of the truck and put a blindfold over my eyes. I had never worn a blindfold before. I was immediately disoriented and utterly afraid. I was afraid to take a step. Afraid of being hit. Just plain afraid.

With a man holding each of my arms, I shuffled through a labyrinth of hallways. Eventually we stopped, and one of the guards ordered me to squat.

I tried. But my legs were too weak, and I collapsed to my knees. Somebody shoved my head down. I figured I was in a place with concrete walls. The floor felt like concrete. The guards' voices echoed when they yelled.

I could tell that there were other prisoners nearby. I could hear them crying and screaming. It sounded as if they were being tortured.

I was so scared I wet my pants. *Oh, Lord,* I thought. *Help me. Please.*

Before long I was forced back up to my feet and pushed somewhere else. Then the blindfold was removed from my eyes. I was standing in front of a fat man seated behind a desk. The desk had nothing on it except a dinged-up bell. The man behind it had a big mustache. In the Arab world, a mustache is a symbol of manhood. The bigger the mustache, the bigger the man.

"Salman Rushdie of Egypt, are you going to cooperate with me?"

I didn't answer.

"We don't want you," he said. "We want the people who helped you try to escape from Egypt."

Still I said nothing.

"If you sit down and tell us the story," the immigration official said, "we can be of great help to you."

"Bring him a cup of tea," he said to his assistant.

"No, thank you, sir," I said.

"Something else to drink?"

"Water, sir."

"Bring him water."

Then he turned back to me. "You talk to me and your problems will go away."

I doubted that.

"Who helped you out of Egypt?"

"I didn't leave Egypt."

He laughed. "Don't be smart. I am talking to you like a friend."

I didn't believe that for a second. In Egyptian security facilities, the men in uniform are not your friend.

I could still hear the sounds of men being tortured on the floor above.

The official and I looked at each other in silence. Then he glanced up at the ceiling, toward the direction of men howling. "Those men," he said, "are much bigger than you."

I didn't doubt it. But God, I told myself, was much bigger than the security official I was facing. I wasn't going to cave in.

"Nobody helped me," I said. "If you want to take my life, it is in your hands."

He pounded the desk. "Hey! You are not listening."

He rang the bell on his desk, and two armed men rushed in.

I jumped to my feet.

"I'm going to send you behind the sun," the official told me. Then he faced the guards. "Give him the good treatment."

"Yes, boss," they said in unison.

They reapplied the blindfold and dragged me out. I had no idea where they were taking me. Eventually, they shoved me down. I landed on what felt like a wool blanket. My ankles and wrists were still restrained. Suddenly I felt some sort of belt or cord being wrapped around my arms and upper body. Then I felt a tingle, immediately followed by an electrical charge. I remember squirming and screaming. But not for long. I lost consciousness pretty quickly.

I'm not sure how long I was out. But when I regained consciousness I was being dragged down a hallway by a couple of guards who were pulling me by a belt that was fastened around my waist. I was no longer blindfolded. I ended up in a cell occupied by another prisoner. Bleeding and too weak to stand, I crawled into a corner and curled up like an abused dog.

I thought about praying. But I didn't. I was too weak, too tired, too far gone. Besides, I told myself, what was the point? God wasn't listening to me anyway. He didn't care about me. Nobody did. I was alone in a cell in the bowels of a government building in Cairo. I was pretty sure I was going to die there. And I didn't care.

After a while, the other prisoner introduced himself. He said he was from Ethiopia. I didn't care where he was from. I didn't feel like talking.

But then he introduced himself. His last name sounded familiar, although I couldn't place it.

"What is your name?" he said.

"Muhammad Awal from Nigeria."

I surprised myself by how easily I reverted to my legal name. I'd been going by Tito since becoming a Christian. That's what all my friends called me too. But at that moment I didn't even think about saying Tito. It was as if my association with Christianity had already faded. I was going back to what I used to be—Muhammad the Muslim.

"I've heard about you," the prisoner said.

That got my attention. After a few more minutes of discussion, I figured out why his last name rang a bell. His sister used to be a regular at one of the nightclubs where I worked as a DJ. She and I were friends.

I couldn't believe that I had ended up in a cell with the brother of a woman I knew from my DJ days. Later that day my cell mate received a visit from an official with the Ethiopian consulate in Egypt. During the visit, my cellmate introduced me to the official. He took pity on my condition and asked what he could do to help. I gave him the address for Dutch's apartment, where I had stashed my old passport in a shoebox, along with a few other personal papers. I asked the official to retrieve my passport and bring it to me. He gave me his word that he would do his best. After he left, my cell mate told me I could count on the official.

My faith was starting to return. So was my guilt. I had given up on God. When things got really dark and desperate, I abandoned hope. But God hadn't given up on me. He hadn't forgotten me. No one other than my captors knew my whereabouts. Only God knew where I was. And in my darkest hour he led me to a cell with a stranger who offered to help me.

I didn't feel worthy of the help. I should have trusted.

Later that day the Ethiopian consulate official returned and slipped me my passport. The next time I was dragged before the top immigration official, I handed him my passport.

"What is this?" he said.

"My passport."

He turned up his hands, and the skin furrowed on his brow. He thumbed through the passport, inspecting each page carefully. There was no exit or entry stamp showing travel to Spain.

"This is a mystery," he said.

"Guard," he yelled.

Two men entered the room. "Take him to the waiting area while I make a phone call," he told them.

Ten minutes later I was ushered back in.

"Are you sure this is your passport?" he asked.

"My picture is in there. It is me."

This ultimately led to my release. But not before some restrictions were imposed. Once a month I had to report to immigration and present my passport. Additionally, I was told my attendance at church with the Mormon congregation in Cairo was limited to one hour each week. No more.

I was not convicted of any crime. In fact, I hadn't even been charged. Yet I was essentially put on probation. This was justice in Egypt.

But at least I was getting out of jail. My leg irons and handcuffs were removed, and I signed a series of documents, pledging that I'd abide by the terms set forth by the immigration official. A couple of hours later I was wandering free on the streets of Cairo. I looked like a vagabond. I felt like one, too. But I didn't care. I was on the street and not in jail.

I headed to Dutch's apartment for a shower, a change of clothes, a meal, and a comfortable couch to sleep on. Later that night it dawned on me. The Egyptian authorities had specifically limited my church attendance to one hour per week. By making me sign papers to that effect, the authorities were implicitly authorizing me to attend a Christian church. Yet there was intense political pressure against Muslims converting to Christianity. And here I was being told I could go to a church that was not registered in Egypt. It didn't make sense.

I couldn't help smelling a rat. Maybe the authorities hoped they'd catch me or some members of my congregation doing something inappropriate. I determined I wouldn't let that happen. No more mistakes.

CHAPTER 25

A NEW NAME

I lived underground for the next year. I didn't go anywhere or do anything other than part-time work as an English tutor and an interpreter. Besides that I attended church for one hour a week. Otherwise, I stayed indoors and did a lot of reading. I felt I was under surveillance, and I was afraid to do anything that would get me in trouble. I just hoped that eventually the authorities would lose interest in me.

As the year dragged on, I felt I was losing my sanity. I had no life. I had no future, either. There was nothing to look forward to. Tutoring and translating were earning me enough money to feed myself. But I had to move into a small apartment with five other Muslim friends just to get by. I was poor, and teaching people to speak English wasn't going to change that.

Money wasn't the only thing I lacked. The closest thing I had to family in Cairo was the members of the Mormon congregation.

They had been far more accepting of me than my own relatives had. But I was withdrawing from them, too. I was afraid that my association with them would endanger them. I didn't want the state security or the police to start harassing people in the church.

I guess I was becoming afraid of a lot of things. The sense of being watched made me paranoid. Everywhere I looked I saw danger, both real and imagined. I couldn't go on living that way. I had to make a change.

I started researching immigration law in Egypt. I was looking for a way out of the country without detection. It occurred to me that a legal name change might just do the trick. I had had a fair amount of experience with helping students change their names. Before dropping out of Al-Azhar, I had assisted numerous Christians to take on a Muslim name. The process was pretty simple.

On April 7, 1991, the paperwork to officially change my legal name from Muhammad Awal to Tito Awal was completed at the Ministry of the Interior. The process had gone smoothly. Technically, I had a new name. But I still had to visit Al-Azhar, because I had come into the country under a student visa that was associated with the university. There were a number of forms that I had to have signed by the school, acknowledging that I was no longer a student there and that my name had been changed. That had to be completed before I could go to the embassy to apply for a passport.

I started sensing a problem at Al-Azhar when the clerk who took my paperwork disappeared. I stood at her window for at least twenty minutes without any sign of her. Eventually someone else came to the window and told me to have a seat.

Nearly two hours later I was still sitting and waiting. Finally, a couple of state security officers showed up behind the counter. Around that time the clerk who had originally taken my paperwork resurfaced. Only she was talking to the security officers. Not a good sign.

They were too far away for me to hear what they were saying. But I could read the expressions on their faces—grave. As the clerk spoke, the officers were nodding their heads. Then the clerk handed papers to the officers. A few minutes later the officers came out to the waiting area and asked me to follow them. One of them was holding my name-change paperwork and my passport.

The next thing I knew I was on my way back to the same building where I had been beaten and jailed one year earlier. I even ended up before the same state security officer that had interrogated me, the one with the oversized mustache. He seemed to take pleasure in having me in his custody again.

"So, Salman Rushdie of Egypt, you are back again," he said, laughing. "I told you we would meet again."

My hands were handcuffed behind my back. Afraid to speak, I stood erect and looked straight ahead.

"Instead of cooperating with us, you are trying to change your name," he said.

He stepped out from behind his desk and started saying things like "You don't like Muhammad's name? You don't want the holy prophet's name?"

He backhanded me across the face. "You took a dog's name. In Egypt, only dogs are called Tito."

He pushed me in the chest, causing me to lose my balance and fall to my knees. "How could you do something so blasphemous?" he said, looking down on me.

With the officer still shouting at me, two guards in combat boots began kicking me. It's a frightening thing to see boots coming at you and be unable to deflect them or protect yourself from them. One blow to my abdomen knocked the wind out of me. I gasped for air. When I regained my breath I cried like I did when my father beat me as a young boy.

The authorities kept me in a cell for a couple of days. Then they put me in a police vehicle and transported me to my apartment.

When we arrived, Egyptian police officers were there. They said they were going to conduct a search.

It was more like a raid. All five of my roommates were taken into custody, and the officers ransacked our apartment. They rifled through desks, removed everything from dresser drawers and closets, and turned over mattresses and furniture cushions. I was never told what they were after. But my personal papers and my books were seized, including my photographs of my mother. I knew I'd never see them again.

Luckily, I had taken my Bible and Book of Mormon to another friend's apartment just a few days earlier. Those surely would have been used against me if they had ended up in the authorities' hands.

My roommates ended up spending one night in jail. Then they were released. But not before being questioned about whether I tried to convert them to Christianity.

It was pretty clear why I was in so much trouble—my religion. The authorities had it in for me because I was a Christian. They were convinced that I was trying to persuade others to do what I had done—convert from Islam.

My roommates denied this, insisting I had never talked to them about Christianity.

They were telling the truth. I had never introduced any of my Muslim roommates to my religious beliefs. The authorities didn't want to believe it, though, and they were determined to prove otherwise.

My roommates stuck to their story. But over the next few weeks, the police interviewed numerous students from Al-Azhar. They told a different story—namely that I had been actively trying to convert people to my new religion.

That was a lie. Not one Al-Azhar student could point to a specific instance where I had approached someone about Christianity. But that didn't matter. The authorities released my acquaintances, and I was sent to a place referred to as the Investigations Prison, where accused criminals were held until they got a hearing.

The jail had a ripe smell of urine. Cockroaches moved along the ceiling. I was put in a giant holding cell with more than sixty other accused criminals who were waiting for their cases to be heard. It was immediately obvious that there was a pecking order in the cell. Within a minute of my entering the lockup, a boy who looked roughly seventeen approached me. "Mabachia," he said.

"What does that mean?" I said.

"Service fee," he said.

"What?"

He put out his empty hand. "Two packs of cigarettes."

"You are hustling me for cigarettes? Are you crazy? I don't have anything."

A husky man in his fifties with blond, curly hair stepped between us. "Leave him alone," he said to the teenager. "He is a foreigner."

Then the man looked at me. "Where are you from?"

"Nigeria."

"The best people," he said.

"Thank you."

He handed me a pack of Marlboro cigarettes.

"I don't smoke," I told him.

"Keep it. You'll need it. In here there is no money. Cigarettes are the currency."

I shoved the pack in my pocket.

"If you need anything, call on me."

This man, I quickly learned, was the captain of the cell. Every cell had a captain, who ran the place and kept the peace.

The cell also had a sheik. At the dinner hour, the sheik called all of us to pray. Everyone sat cross-legged on the ground. The sheik sat on a mattress.

"God is great," he said.

"Amen," everyone repeated.

"God is displeased with us," the sheik said.

"Amen!" the men shouted.

This went on for twenty minutes. Then the sheik distributed dates. They were large, red, and soft, a clear sign that they had come from Iraq. I ate a few. They tasted as sweet as honey.

Then the evening meal was distributed. Everyone received a small box containing a piece of roasted chicken, yogurt, and cucumber salad. Everyone devoured his food. For a beverage we were each given eight ounces of soda.

While I was in jail, the court assigned a lawyer to represent me. But he wasn't much of a lawyer. He never came around, leaving me desperate for help. Fortunately, one of my old roommates tracked down an Egyptian woman who was a friend of mine. My roommate told her that I was in police custody and that I was being persecuted for my religious beliefs. This woman was a Muslim. But she knew a couple of the members of the Mormon congregation in Cairo. One day she visited me at the jail, and I slipped her a handwritten note addressed to the leader of the Mormon congregation. The note explained my situation and asked for the church's help. She promised to deliver it for me.

I was sure help would come. But it never did. I don't know if it was because my note was never delivered or members of the congregation chose to stay away. The bottom line was that no one from the church came to visit me.

But Dutch did. I was allowed to see him for only a few minutes. I was in a big pen with scores of other prisoners, separated from our visitors by a barrier made of chicken wire. Women were weeping for their husbands. Cigarette smoke permeated the air.

"How are you holding up?" he asked.

"I pray to God that I'll get out of here."

"I've got some news."

"What?"

"I'm going back to Holland."

"You're leaving?"

"My time here in Egypt is finished," he said.

I was so depressed I didn't know what to say.

"I will keep in touch with you," he said.

"You're one of the best friends I ever had," I said.

"You truly are the best of people," he said.

I stood frozen like a block of ice, watching him walk out of the jail. I felt too discouraged and alone to cry.

After nearly nine months in detention, I finally was taken before a panel of judges. The courtroom was packed with prisoners. We were shackled and haggard. For a brief period I was placed in a cage with metal bars. There were a few other prisoners in there with me. I felt like a zoo animal while I was in the cage. The court officers treated us like animals, too.

I was on my own—a foreigner with no money, no connections, and a poor excuse for a lawyer. And I was facing the Egyptian legal system.

My lawyer spoke to me for less than a minute before my case was called.

I was charged with drug possession and falsifying my identity. I didn't know what to say. I had never used illegal drugs in my life. I didn't even hang around people who used drugs. On one occasion a couple of years earlier I had been with some friends who smoked hashish. I became so sick and feverish just from breathing the smoke that I never went near the stuff again. Yet there I was being accused of using cocaine and heroin.

I was anticipating charges for falsifying papers, but the authorities didn't go after me for that. The reason they were after me was my conversion to Christianity. Why else would they bring up my affiliation with the Mormon faith every time they interrogated me? In the eyes of hard-line Muslims, that was the most serious crime of all.

My enemies were determined to see me die in prison.

My memory of the court hearing is a blur. I don't remember

much of the proceeding. The judges yelled. My lawyer cowered. I remained virtually silent. It seemed like the outcome was a foregone conclusion. I figured I was going to be sent away for a few years. No way around it.

Mostly I remember the atmosphere in the courtroom. It was crowded with accused criminals. I was let out of the cage and allowed to wait with other prisoners. I sat on the floor in a sea of men. The man next to me was a drug baron from Nigeria. We were chained together for a brief time. He had a high-priced lawyer. At one point the baron offered his lawyer's services to me. But I politely declined, saying I preferred to let the Lord provide. The drug baron nodded and grinned. I think he thought I was pretty naïve.

I guess I was. But at the same time, I knew that doubting God wasn't wise either.

I was in the middle of a silent prayer when I heard my case called over the loud speaker. I stood up and pushed my way through the crowed toward the front of the courtroom. The judge pronounced a guilty verdict and ordered me to serve a life sentence.

His words just hung in the air.

Life?

At first it didn't sink in. I wanted to bury my face in my hands. But I couldn't even do that. My hands were cuffed behind my back.

Instead, I just let the tears flow down my cheeks. I didn't care who saw me. I told myself: *The Lord knows best.*

But at that moment I wasn't sure I believed that anymore. I was trying to cling to my faith. But I felt like a man hanging by his fingertips from the edge of a high rock cliff. I lacked the strength to pull myself up. And there was no one around to lend me a hand.

By the time I was led out of the courtroom and loaded into a vehicle to transport me to prison, all I could see was gloom and darkness. I had been a Christian for less than two years. I was thirty-one years old. And I was going off to spend the rest of my life in prison.

A NEW NAME

The Israelites spent forty years in the desert of Sinai before reaching the promised land, but it looked as if I was never leaving.

It would have been so much easier if I had just remained a Muslim and pretended to believe.

CHAPTER 26

THE INFIDEL

Fyodor Dostoevsky is famously quoted as having said, "The degree of civilization in a society can be judged by entering its prisons." I was about to find out for myself just how uncivilized things were in Egypt's prison system. I was sent to Tora Prison, which is actually a big complex of five prisons on the outskirts of Cairo. Over the years it has housed some of Egypt's most notorious political prisoners and terrorists. Islamist Ayman al-Zawahiri was held there until 1984. He later became the number two man in Al-Qaeda. More recently, al-Qaeda founding member Sayyid Imam Al-Sharif was taken into custody in Yemen after the 9/11 attacks in the United States and later transferred to Tora to serve a life sentence.

Conditions inside Tora are notoriously bad. Food deprivation, torture, and the withholding of medical care from sick and injured prisoners are common. Amnesty International and the Human Rights Centre for the Assistance of Prisoners have each issued scathing reports documenting abuse and neglect of inmates. A British prisoners' rights group reported the case of an inmate who was electrocuted, hanged upside down, whipped with electrical wire, and forced to lick his cell floor clean.

I didn't know all of this at the time, but I did know I was headed to a bad place.

It was just after 4 p.m. when I entered the prison gates to be processed. The Muslim inmates were praying. Most of the prisoners were Muslims.

All the new arrivals were herded into a big room that resembled a warehouse. Roll call was taken. Then we were ordered to put our hands against the wall and spread our legs. Guards strip-searched us while a constable walked behind with a leather switch that he used to beat us across the back. There was no particular reason for him to whip us. He did it simply because he could.

Then our heads were shaved. The barber was a beast. He used dull clippers and seemed to take pride in leaving little cuts and gouges all over our heads. Luckily I didn't have a mustache. Those were cut off. In the prison, only the guards had mustaches, which showed their superiority over the inmates.

Eventually, we were given our cell assignments. Prisoners were housed in different sections, depending on the type of crimes they had committed. I found out that I was going to the section that housed domestic terrorists and convicted members of the Muslim Brotherhood. I knew I was in for it.

Schoolteacher Hassan al-Banna founded the Brotherhood in Egypt in 1928. Its mission is to resist the secularism of Islamic nations. Its motto is "Allah is our objective. The Prophet is our leader. Qur'an is our law. Jihad is our way. Dying in the way of Allah is our highest hope."

Al-Banna, who has been described by Jewish organizations as a devout admirer of Hitler and the Nazi regime, set up branches of the Brotherhood throughout the Middle East during World War II.

It was banned in Egypt after a member of the Brotherhood assassinated the Egyptian prime minister in 1948, but it was legalized again in 1964. Members of the Brotherhood were blamed for the assassination of Egyptian president Anwar Sadat in 1981.

When Egyptian president Hosni Mubarak came to power after Sadat's assassination, he and his regime targeted the Muslim Brotherhood. The prisons were full of its members. Not all of them deserved to be there, but the fanatical ones had a reputation for violence, especially toward a Muslim who had turned his back on his religion to become a Christian.

Silently, I started praying for a guardian angel. Growing up, I had been taught to believe in angels. According to the teachings of Islam, angels are spirit beings created from light, while Adam—or man—was created from clay. Every man, according to Islamic belief, has two angels over him, one on the right and one on the left. The one on the right records a person's good deeds. The one on the left records sins.

Years earlier I had abandoned the belief that angels recorded good and bad deeds. That seemed more like folklore than anything else. But I never stopped believing in angels. And I was begging for one to show up at Tora quick.

The guards unlocked a sliding cell door that led to a common area packed with fanatic Islamic terrorists of one sort or another. They were all looking at me.

"This is the Al-Azhar student who converted to Christianity," one of the guards announced, shoving me through the door. "This is the infidel."

There are a lot of details I don't remember about that day. But the guard's exact words are etched in my mind like a scar that never fades from your face.

The guards barely had time to exit and lock things down before a throng of inmates converged on me. I can't say for sure how many of them came at me. They looked like a pack of hungry wolves, and

I was the rabbit. The hatred in their eyes terrified me. I could hardly swallow. It felt like I had a bone in my throat.

I dropped to my knees and wrapped my arms around my bald head as they pummeled me with fists and feet. With my arms protecting my face and head, my ribs were fully exposed to the blows of their kicks. I figured I was a goner.

Then I heard a voice.

"Who is that?" a man called out in Arabic.

The inmates stopped attacking me. I was afraid to uncover my head. Slowly, I glanced up at a distinguished-looking man in his forties. He was dressed in a robe. He looked like a cleric. He repeated his question about my identity.

One of the inmates told him I was the infidel from Al-Azhar.

The beating resumed.

"Let the boy alone," the distinguished man said sharply.

The inmates stopped again.

At that point I had no idea what was going on or what would happen next.

"My boy," the man said to me in a soft tone.

I looked up at him again.

He used his arms to motion me to come to him.

My attackers backed away from me. Crying and shaking, I rose to my feet. My clothes were torn, and welts were already popping up on parts of my hands, arms, back, and neck.

Hesitant, I stumbled toward the man. He removed a handkerchief from his pocket and handed it to me. I wiped tears from my cheeks and patted a few of the bloody abrasions on my skin.

"Do you speak English?" the man asked, continuing in his thick Arabic accent.

"Yes," I replied in Arabic.

The man nodded. That was the answer he wanted.

"Can you teach me English?" he continued.

I nodded.

He grinned. "Come, my son," he said, motioning for me to follow him.

None of the inmates said a word as I walked behind the man toward his cell. It was different from the other cells. Most cells were filthy and barren, lacking even a cot, never mind pillows and sheets. It wasn't uncommon to see rodent feces on the floors, either. But his cell was clean and orderly. It was larger and had furniture: a bed, a table, and a chair.

He invited me to sit down on the floor. Then he turned to a younger inmate who appeared to be a lieutenant of sorts. The older man instructed the younger man to bring me tea.

I told the man that I didn't drink tea. Under the circumstances, I'm not sure why I bothered to say that, especially since my mouth was so dry that it felt like I had been chewing on cotton.

He brought me water instead. I downed it like a dog.

Staring silently, the man sat opposite me, his legs crossed. He was husky and had a long, thick beard that was dark with shades of gray. It was another outward sign that indicated he was different from the other inmates. No other inmates had facial hair. His skin complexion was light. All the inmates clearly revered him. Even the prison guards paid him deference.

I wanted to know his name. But I was too afraid to ask. And he didn't volunteer it.

"Take a breath," he said. "Feel at home. Once you enter this cage, you must forget what is behind it. We are all here for one another."

Uneasy and scared, I nodded.

"So you can speak English very well?" he asked.

"Yes."

"Where have you taught English?"

"At the International Living Language Institute in Cairo. It's a school commissioned by the British for teaching English. I also did translation work for an English-speaking foreign journalist."

"Do you need instruction books?"

"Just one."

At his request I supplied the name of the book to the inmate who served as the older man's lieutenant. The lieutenant assured me that the textbook would arrive within a couple of days. The older man nodded his approval and asked if I needed anything else smuggled into prison. I told him no.

While we were conversing, a few other inmates approached. "Imam," one of them said in a respectful tone, "how can you do this? This guy is an infidel."

The title *imam* got my attention. Most of the inmates in my cell block were Shiite Muslims. And Shiite Muslims consider an imam to be a divinely appointed spiritual leader. He told the inmates that they were to leave me alone. They didn't like it. But I knew they would obey. A Shiite does not go against his imam—ever. They walked off with their heads down. I was safe.

I couldn't help thinking that my silent prayer for a guardian angel had been answered. God had chosen an imprisoned imam to save me. My faith in Christ was starting to come back in a big way.

That first night in prison I hardly slept. I had my own cell. All the prisoners in my section had single cells. It was a bit like being in solitary confinement. That was just fine with me. I wanted to be alone.

I lay on my prison-issued gray wool blanket staring at the ceiling. I couldn't stop replaying the day's events over and over in my mind. So often in life we think we've got things figured out, only to find out otherwise.

When I got up the next morning, a guard appeared at my cell. He told me that he was taking me to have breakfast with the imam. I didn't ask questions. I just followed the guard.

I eventually discovered that there was something peculiar about this particular prison guard. Almost all of the guards in the prison were Muslims. But the guard who accompanied me that morning was a Copt. He didn't reveal that until much later. But during my imprisonment, he and I ultimately became friends. Although he couldn't show it outwardly, this guard had sympathy for me and my situation. As a Coptic Christian, he knew what it was like to be a persecuted minority. So he looked out for me in little ways. It was another sign that God was watching out for me.

On that first morning when he escorted me to breakfast with the imam, he asked me if I knew the imam's name.

I told him I had no idea.

The guard leaned in and whispered the man's name.

I froze. I recognized it immediately. He was a founding member of the Islamic jihad group that had assassinated Egyptian president Anwar Sadat. He was one of Egypt's most famous political prisoners, credited with helping mastermind the assassination plot.

An ominous feeling swept over me. I had read stories about this man. According to published reports, he held the rank of colonel in the Egyptian military at the time of Sadat's assassination. He had worked in intelligence, which contributed to the belief that he had been behind the unpredictable plan for military personnel to fire on the presidential stand during a military parade held on the eve of Egypt's Armed Forces Day. He had denied the charge, insisting he had only supplied the ammunition. But the Cairo criminal court had sentenced him to life behind bars for his role in the attack. As a result of that conviction, he emerged as a leading figure in the Egyptian Jihad Organization.

No wonder the militant Islamic inmates practically worshipped him. And now this same man was an imam and my ticket to protection in prison in exchange for my teaching him English. The image of a guardian angel no longer seemed appropriate. It was hard picturing an assassin as heaven sent.

I didn't know whether to feel grateful or guilty. Over breakfast, I thought, *I'm breaking bread with one of the most notorious criminals in the Middle East, a man who had helped take out a world leader.*

But he had saved my life. And if I cut ties with him, I would not survive long in a wing of Islamic jihadists and fundamentalists.

My situation was complicated. I tried to figure out what God wanted me to do, but I received no inspiration, no clear signal. So I went with my gut instinct—life is better than death. It was no accident, I told myself, that I had crossed paths with this man when I did. Nor did it make sense for me to judge him for his past. I decided I would follow through with the plan to be his English teacher.

CHAPTER 27

THE COMPROMISE

The manual for teaching English made its way into the prison quickly, and I immediately started teaching. My sessions with the imam always took place toward mid-afternoon. His mornings were tied up leading prayers, preaching, and holding meetings. He was the busiest inmate in the prison.

It would be three o'clock or thereabouts when he got around to sitting down with me. We'd work for about an hour. Then he liked to go for a stroll inside the prison. His pace was leisurely. He'd talk and I'd listen. This was his daily routine.

The imam had opinions on a wide range of topics: history, philosophy, the military, and world affairs, to name a few. Listening to him was a bit like listening to a philosopher. But whenever he got onto the subject of religion, he was interested in what I had to say. He respected the way I had been raised, and he appreciated my command of the Qur'an, as well as my background in Islamic studies. Early on, he asked me about Christ.

Free to speak my mind, I explained why I had accepted Jesus as my Savior. I started out by saying that all of us are imperfect. All of us have flaws. It's part of being human. Ultimately, we are all in need of redemption. Only God is capable of offering redemption. Christ is the Son of God—the Only Begotten—and he is our redeemer. He was born to die for mankind.

The imam listened before boiling it all down to a simple conclusion. If what I was saying was true, that would mean replacing Allah with Christ as the Supreme Being.

That was a big and dangerous statement. I was tentative when it came to admitting that I believed it. At the same time, I couldn't deny his logic. I told him that his interpretation of my belief was correct. Then I held my breath, afraid of what he might say next.

But he responded with a query: How could I do that?

He didn't ask how I could believe that way. He asked how I could do that. *Do* is an action word. The action he was referring to was my decision to change faiths. Muslims, especially extreme ones, don't accept change. I suppose all of us are that way to some degree. But in orthodox Islam, change just isn't done. Not when it comes to beliefs and rituals.

He wanted to know more about my conversion. I liked telling him. I found it uplifting, which was a feeling I rarely experienced in prison.

Still, it was difficult to adequately explain the convictions that were deep in my soul. Faith is something you feel, not something intellectual. Defining it can be like trying to describe the taste of salt. You have to experience it to understand.

The imam had deeply held spiritual convictions of his own. But he had a practical side. He'd listen to me and then ask such things as, "Don't you know what you face?"

I told him that after what I'd gone through, I had a pretty good idea of the consequences of my decision. I'd been living with hostility for two years. I think perhaps he admired that about me. Or he felt sorry for me. I'm not sure which.

Some days I purposely kept the conversation light. For instance, on one occasion I told him that the Qur'an has more to say about Mary the mother of Jesus than the Bible does. He found that hard to believe. But he had never read the New Testament. He knew that I had read it more than once.

At his invitation, I shared with him the few passages from the Bible that discuss Mary. Then I quoted the references to Mary from the Qur'an. The imam was surprised that the Bible said less. He was also surprised by my fluency in both books of scripture. That got him onto a topic of far greater interest to him—the Book of Mormon.

He was somewhat familiar with the Book of Mormon before he met me. He also knew about other aspects of the Mormon faith prior to our paths crossing. He certainly knew about Joseph Smith. He was aware, for instance, that Joseph Smith was credited with founding The Church of Jesus Christ of Latter-day Saints and that he had been assassinated in America by other so-called Christians. He thought that was pretty telling. I did too.

Eventually he asked me if I really believed the Joseph Smith story.

Joseph Smith claimed that he was confused about which church to join when he was a fourteen-year-old boy living in upstate New York in the early 1800s. Then he read a passage from the book of James in the New Testament, which stated that any man who lacked wisdom should ask God. The passage went on to say that if man asked in faith, nothing wavering, God would answer. Prompted by these words, Joseph claimed that he then went into the woods to offer a simple prayer. The result was a vision that included a visit from God the Father and his Only Begotten Son, Jesus Christ. Both personages spoke to Joseph, with God pointing to his Son and telling Joseph to hear him.

Joseph Smith also claimed that an angel later visited him. He said that the angel directed him to a set of golden plates that was buried in a hillside in Palmyra, New York. The plates contained a record of two great civilizations, one of which came from Jerusalem in 600 B.C. and later separated into two nations known as Nephites and Lamanites. Joseph translated the ancient writings from these plates. His translation was published in 1830 as the Book of Mormon, which, among other things, tells of Christ's visit to the Nephites after his resurrection.

Without hesitation, I told the imam that I believed Joseph Smith saw what he said he saw. I also told him that I believed the Book of Mormon was the word of God.

The idea that God visited a prophet wasn't hard for the imam to accept. Neither was the notion of an angel visiting the earth to deliver a sacred book of scripture to a man. After all, Muslims believe that God visited Muhammad and called him to be a prophet. That's basically what Mormons say happened to Joseph Smith. Muslims also believe that God delivered a sacred book to Muhammad. It's pretty similar to what Joseph Smith claimed. So the concepts weren't outlandish to him. He just believed those experiences were exclusive to Islam and didn't happen in modern times to Joseph Smith or anyone else. In that respect, he wasn't much different from most Christians who reject the founding tenets of Mormonism.

I was impressed that he listened to me. He didn't agree with me, but he didn't criticize or condemn me. He didn't try to talk me out of my beliefs, either. Nor did I try to influence his beliefs.

CHAPTER 28

BETTER LEFT UNSAID

I n prison the days tend to blend together. Every day is the same. You lose track of time. That's because it doesn't matter what time or day it is. There is nothing to do and nowhere to go.

Many of the prisoners in my cell block killed time watching hours of mindless television. There was one television in the entire block, which forced everyone to watch the same programming. No, thank you. It's bad enough that your body goes to waste behind bars. I couldn't stand the thought of my mind turning to mush, too.

Tutoring the imam was a great outlet. Besides exercising my mind by teaching him English, we had a steady stream of stimulating dialogue on other matters. Unfortunately, that lasted for only a little over three months. Then he just stopped showing up at our appointed time. It wasn't that English was too hard for him to learn. The man had the intelligence to learn any language he wanted. For some reason, he just stopped the lessons. He never explained why, and I didn't ask.

But before the imam discontinued the lessons, I worked up the courage to ask him to help me obtain a copy of the Book of Mormon and the Bible. He seemed capable of smuggling just about anything into prison. I figured he could get me a couple of books.

I made the request after I had been in enough conversations with him to realize that my faith was stronger than I had estimated. Or maybe I was just getting stronger as the opposition increased. Either way, I was increasingly proud to count myself a disciple of Christ.

He went along with my request. He told me to write a letter to someone on the outside who was capable of turning over the two books I had requested. I wrote the letter and delivered it to the imam. Weeks later a Book of Mormon and Bible were smuggled into the prison. I don't know who did what or how the books got in. But the day that I received them, I knelt down in the darkness of my cell and silently thanked God. I was seeing miracles. How else could I describe the fact that an Islamic terrorist was willing to help a Muslim infidel get Christian scriptures into the prison?

The fact that the imam was willing to have a message delivered in my behalf helped me appreciate a belief that runs deep in Mormon culture that God works in mysterious ways. If anybody's situation was living proof of this, mine was. One minute I was being beaten and mocked by Islamic extremists for becoming a Christian. The next minute the spiritual leader of these extremists—a man accused of plotting to kill the Egyptian president—had rescued me. I had to believe the Lord's hand was in all this.

The one thing I never discussed with the imam was the assassination of Anwar Sadat. I made a point of steering clear of mentioning how much I liked Sadat and what he stood for. The hatred toward the former president remained hot among Islamic fundamentalist inmates. Anytime his name surfaced in prison, the inmates in my section would spit and become animated in their anger. All of them believed that Sadat had sold out the Arabs to the Americans.

I often wanted to broach this subject with the imam. But I didn't. I figured that if he wanted to discuss the Sadat assassination, he would bring it up. He never did.

That was the one thing about him that I could never come to terms with. But I recognized that he probably never came to terms with my departure from Islam for Christianity.

Yet he didn't hold that against me. Nor did I judge him for his past. I guess that is one of the only redeeming qualities of prison life. It forces you to overlook people's flaws and find ways to accept and befriend people you would otherwise shun.

After I stopped tutoring the imam, I'd still see him from time to time. Fortunately, he remained friendly toward me. But as soon as the lessons were discontinued, I requested a transfer to another part of the prison. It took a little while, but I ended up being moved to an area that housed all the foreign prisoners.

The good news was that I was no longer with all the convicted terrorists and radical militants. The bad news was that I no longer had my own cell. Each cell in my new wing held eighteen inmates.

CHAPTER 29

PRISON LIFE

Until I lost my freedom I took for granted the simple pleasures
in life. Going to the market to pick up my favorite food or beverage, meeting a friend for dinner, listening to music or watching a
film, going for a walk along the Nile on a warm night, telephoning
a friend just to say hello, or holding a woman's hand—none of these
are options in prison.

We were fed slop that was fit only for pigs. Sometimes we were
so hungry that we ate like pigs, using our hands and competing for
rations of things that we'd never dare eat under any other circumstances. It's amazing what you'll swallow when you're starving.

There was no music whatsoever. No movies, either. The arts
were absent in confinement, which made brutal men more so.

Late-night walks were out of the question, as prisoners were always locked down by 5 p.m. The entire time I was there I never saw
the moon or stars. If you go that long without seeing the nighttime

233

sky, you start to forget what it looks like. Even in the daytime we weren't allowed outside. Tora had a reputation for preventing inmates from getting fresh air for months or even years at a time.

Calls to friends were not allowed, either. Visits were restricted. Prison officials often denied entry to visitors, and when they were admitted, the visits were usually limited to fifteen minutes. The visits took place in a crowded room, and between the noise and the presence of armed guards, the nature of the conversations was pretty superficial.

As for holding a woman's hand, well, there were no women in our section. The prison guards were all men, too. Very few women were admitted as visitors. Something changes in a man when he goes for years without seeing any women. And it's not a healthy change.

Those are some of the milder downsides of prison. Beatings and torture were much more severe. The beatings were usually one or more inmates taking down another inmate. The only time that happened to me was the day I arrived at Tora Prison. From then on I managed to avoid confrontation.

Torture, on the other hand, was inflicted by the guards, not the inmates. Sometimes it was used to extract information from an inmate. Occasionally, torture was used as punishment for insubordination. But most of the time inmates were tortured for no particular reason.

I knew guys who'd had electrodes attached to their genitals, nipples, and even their tongues. I knew guys whose arms were stretched wide by ropes and left in that position for hours. I knew guys who'd been beaten almost to death just for the amusement of prison guards.

All of my personal experience with torture took place before my incarceration. Once I entered Tora, I was left alone for the most part. I was slapped here and there, verbally abused, and denied food and water now and again. But I was spared any really harsh treatment. In the beginning this was due to my association with the imam. But after I left him and ended up in a general prison population with other foreigners, I was able to navigate around trouble.

Still, I saw and heard a lot. There was a time when my cell was one floor directly below a chamber that was used to torture inmates. We called it the death chamber because we were told that more than one inmate had died there. I hated living beneath that room.

The terrible things that went on above me always seemed to take place at night. I went to sleep to the sounds of terror on more than one occasion. It's a hopeless feeling to hear a man screaming in pain while you are unable to go to his aid. It's even worse when a woman screams. There were no female inmates in our section. But occasionally female inmates were brought from another part of the prison complex for torture or interrogation on the floor above our cell block. One night a female prisoner was to be hanged. For the entire day leading up to her execution, dozens of women wailed at the prison gates. Muslims sometimes hire women to mourn. In this case it did no good. The woman was hanged just the same.

I still feel guilty for being unable to do anything to stop it.

In my new prison section I had to get used to new protocols. With eighteen inmates assigned to a cell, each cell had a captain. Captains were chosen by seniority. The inmate who had been in the cell the longest became the captain and was responsible for maintaining order. That was an essential function considering the space restrictions inside the cell. Each inmate had personal space that amounted to about sixteen inches by less than three feet. That's all the real estate one had for reading, performing Muslim prayers, and sleeping.

Bedtime was when lack of space posed the biggest challenge. Since there were no beds, we slept on the floor and used the head-to-toe rule. My cell had three rows with six inmates in each row. I was in the middle row. So I had an inmate's feet just above my head and another inmate's head almost touching my toes. Since I prefer to sleep on my side, I also had an inmate lying parallel to me both behind me and in front of me. This arrangement gave literal meaning to the expression *packed like sardines*.

Besides making sure that no inmate infringed on another inmate's sleeping space, captains were also responsible for making sure that the toilet was maintained. Since the cells didn't have plumbing, we didn't have a traditional toilet. We had a hole in the floor. It was located near the door to the cell and was about ten inches deep, with an opening just big enough for an inmate to squat over. There were more traditional toilets in the common prison area. But we were not allowed out of our cells after 5 p.m., not even to use the bathroom.

Needless to say, the hole in the floor got a lot of use between the dinner hour and morning. With eighteen men sharing one hole, the odor got pretty ripe. It was critical that the area be cleaned each morning. We were assigned this duty on a rotating basis. Every eighteenth day was my turn. The cell captain made sure no one missed his turn.

In the middle of the night I was awakened by the realization that someone had his hands on me. Because of how close we slept together, I was used to feeling other inmates' bodies rub up or bump against mine, but this was different. Someone was trying to work my pants down below my waist. I screamed and rolled over to find the captain lying next to me with his genitals fully exposed. I started shouting and beating him with my fists. Within seconds everyone in the cell was awake, and a melee ensued. The commotion woke up inmates in nearby cells. Within minutes, guards were on the scene.

The captain and I were hauled to an interrogation office. The captain denied my allegation. But other inmates had seen him with his pants down. The guards knew that. Before long I was sent back to my cell. The captain was sent to a dark room, where he remained for two months as punishment.

It didn't take me long to realize that my encounter that night was not so unusual.

On another occasion, for example, I was accosted in the showers. As prisoners we all showered together. The shower stalls had no doors or walls. Only a narrow knee wall separated one shower space from the next.

One morning I had my eyes closed while I shampooed my head. That's when I felt a man press up against me from behind. Alarmed, I spun around, shoved him off me, and began shouting at him. The guy was in his late fifties, but I started beating on him nonetheless. Other inmates came to his defense, pulling me off the guy and saying he was just mistaken or confused, as if he didn't know what he was doing. There was no doubt in my mind that he had known what he was doing.

My violent reaction to these advances earned me a reputation that protected me from further advances. The younger prisoners—inmates who were seventeen or eighteen—weren't so fortunate. They were much more afraid and therefore much more vulnerable. Some of them were raped. Others tacitly consented by not resisting. I have no way of knowing how many of these young men had experienced a homosexual encounter prior to prison. But most of them became pretty familiar with homosexual activity during their incarceration. That's a taboo subject in the Arab world. But the Egyptian prisons are full of Muslim men engaging in it.

CHAPTER 30

CHANGING
PLACES

W e can dig a tunnel," one of the inmates in my section whispered.

"No," another inmate said. "That would take too long."

The hushed conversation was between an engineer and an electrician. The first time I heard them talking, I wasn't sure what they meant by a tunnel. But they were part of a group of Muslim extremists who hated Mubarak and opposed the Egyptian government. Some of these inmates were former soldiers in the Egyptian army. Others were tradesmen. Some were just common thieves. They shared a fanatical view that they were the true followers of Islam and that the Egyptian government was acting against them. And they were planning an escape. They had even been smuggling tools and explosives into the prison.

"D-Day is coming," one of them told me at one point.

I tried to stay clear of those conversations.

"We want you to come with us," another of them told me.

Just the idea of a prison escape terrified me. I was convinced that it would never work. If it happened, everyone in our section would be put at risk. Guilt by association is common in prison. In the case of an attempted jailbreak, the guards would not be interested in the particulars. They were sure to severely abuse anybody and everybody. That was their way of sending a message and maintaining order.

At night, when the lights were out and all of us were lying in the dark, trying to fall asleep, I would pray silently. "God, please spare me from this plan. I don't want any more trouble."

I did that night after night. It was a feeble prayer, but I didn't really know what to ask for. On November 4, 1994, I awoke to the voice of a guard reading names off a clipboard. When I heard my name, I was scared. All I could think was that the plot had been uncovered, and I had somehow been connected with it.

I turned to a fellow inmate. "What is this about?"

"Transfers," he said.

"I heard my name."

"Congratulations."

I approached the guard with the clipboard. "My name is on that list," I told him.

He ran his finger down the paper. "Yes," he said. "You are going to Kanater Prison." Then he put out this hand. "Give me cigarettes."

Customarily, a tip of one pack of cigarettes was in order for something like this. I was so thrilled to be going somewhere else that I handed him two packs. He smiled. "You leave in an hour," he said.

My cell mates were as shocked as I was. They bombarded me with questions as I packed up my possessions.

"How did you do it?"

"Who do you know?"

"Was it someone at the embassy?

A chill ran through me. I felt a power at work in my life. I was convinced that God was behind my transfer.

Weeks after leaving Tora I heard through the prison grapevine that an escape had been attempted there. It failed miserably because someone had apparently tipped off the prison officials in advance. More than one inmate died, I was told. Many were brutally beaten. I would have been right in the middle of it.

On my first day at Kanater I met an inmate who was an electrician. He got along well with the guards because they often relied on him to fix things. The guy could fix just about anything, electrical or otherwise. When I told him my name, he said he had heard stories about me. Word travels fast in the prisons, and apparently my reputation as a Muslim who had converted to Christianity had gotten around.

"I need to introduce you to José Juan," he said.

"Who is this José Juan?" I asked.

"He is from Spain. He had a medical background."

"I think I have heard of this José," I said. "I heard about him in Tora. Is he the guy who helps sick people in prison?"

"Yes. A lot of guys here have health problems. José uses his medical background to help as much as he can."

"I do want to meet him."

"You will meet him. Every Friday there is a group of us from the prison that gets together to discuss politics, science, art, anything. Here, if you don't do something, you get crazy."

"I know."

"So we've put together a group of guys who are intellectuals. José is in the group."

I nodded.

"Would you like to join us?"

"Yes."

"We meet after Friday prayer."

The first Friday that I was in Kanater I met José. When most of the inmates went to Friday prayer, we stayed behind. I saw a man about five foot eight in height with a slim build and a pointed nose. He had a look about him that I can only describe as good and friendly, qualities that are hard to describe but easy to spot in prison because they are so rare.

"I am Tito Awal," I told him.

"Yes. I have heard about you. I am José Juan. But around here they call me Sheik Abdalla. Or Abdalla for short."

"You are a sheik?"

"No. I am a Christian like you, my friend. They call me sheik because of this." He pointed to his exceptionally long hair and long beard.

I knew we were going to get along.

"What did you do before prison?" I asked.

"I was on my way to becoming a doctor. I had just graduated from medical school in Spain when I got arrested here in Cairo."

"Why were you arrested?"

"My cousin and I had traveled to India. We were on our way home and changing planes in Cairo. We were apprehended at the airport and charged with drug smuggling. I have never smuggled drugs, but the authorities wouldn't listen."

"So your cousin is in here, too?"

"No. He was HIV positive and was granted amnesty."

"What is your sentence?"

"Life. What about you? What's your story?"

"I was a student at Al-Azhar. I was supposed to become a cleric. That was my father's plan for me, anyway. While in Egypt I drifted away from Islam. Eventually I embraced Christianity. That's when my problems started."

"How did you end up here?"

"Like you, I was charged with drug dealing. I've done a lot of stupid things, but I never did that."

241

"Don't we make a good pair," José said. "An aspiring doctor and an aspiring cleric both sitting in prison, falsely accused of peddling drugs."

There were eleven inmates per cell at Kanater. Each cell had one red brick stovetop with an electrical heating element for cooking and one pot. Each cell had a single transom window high above the iron door. The window opening had chicken wire instead of glass. There was also a tiny window at eye level on the door. The walls were concrete. Each cell also had a knee wall in the corner opposite the door. Behind the knee wall was a hole in the floor with a bowl in it. That was our toilet. It had a crude flushing mechanism. There was also a water spigot.

Space was so tight that we used our index finger to mark out our sleeping space at night. We still slept head to toe, but the width of our sleeping area was limited to ten finger lengths, or roughly twenty inches. Sleeping this way was nearly impossible. That's why a lot of inmates took drugs to sedate themselves at night. The drugs came in tiny pills that the inmates would grind to a powder and swallow with water just before bedtime. Prison guards slipped them to inmates in exchange for cigarettes.

The whole system was pretty corrupt. Each inmate had a credit account. Family or friends could put money on an inmate's account, enabling inmates to purchase food and other essentials at the prison cafeteria. The prison would issue a credit slip—we called them prison bonds—that were a substitute for money. The bonds were exchanged at the cafeteria for items. Cigarettes were by far the hottest selling commodities in the prison cafeteria.

For one pack of cigarettes an inmate could obtain three so-called sleeping tablets from a prison guard. This was a moneymaking proposition for the guards. At that time, the street value of a pack of cigarettes was close to two Egyptian pounds. Yet the guards were buying one hundred sleeping tablets for one Egyptian pound. By trading three tablets for one pack of cigarettes, the guards could obtain sixty-six dollars' worth of cigarettes from one dollar's worth of pills.

It was a racket that never went away because many of the inmates became addicted to the pills. I avoided them because they weren't really sleeping pills. Who knows what they were, or where they came from?

Although I managed to stay clear of negative health effects of the pills, I developed a skin disease on my hands. At first it looked like a heat rash. Then bumps surfaced on my fingers and the palms of my hands. Then a yellow liquid started leaking from the bumps. It left a burning sensation that was unbearable. Eventually, the drainage stopped, and the bumps bled. My hands looked as if I had run them over a cheese grater. The same thing happened to my toes.

José talked to the prison guards, and I was permitted to see the prison doctor, who furnished me with injections. I hated needles. Fortunately, José offered to do the injections for me. He came into my cell to do it.

"In the arm or the backside?" he asked.

I undid my belt and pulled down my trousers and underwear. Then I closed my eyes and ground my teeth.

"Okay," he said. "Pull up your trousers."

"It is finished?"

"Yes."

"You sure? I didn't feel anything."

He showed me the empty syringe. "I'm finished."

My cell mates laughed. "José has the magic touch," one of them said.

For ten days José injected me twice a day. Eventually, my hands and feet cleared up.

I had been at Kanater for about a year when José and I were talking one Friday afternoon. "You always seem to smile," I said. "How do you do it?"

"You know something, Tito?" he said. "No Spanish prisoner has been held in an Egyptian prison longer than I have."

"This is true?"

"Yes. That is true."

"Wow."

"The government of Spain has asked President Mubarak to re-mand me to Spain on more than one occasion."

"Why are you still here?"

"The requests have gone unanswered."

"That's what I mean. How are you so upbeat?"

"The more I focus on other people's problems, the less I think about my own," he said.

Before being incarcerated I had never suffered any serious health problems. I seldom got sick. My blood pressure was normal. And my weight always remained pretty consistent—right around 185. But nearly ten years in prison had done a number on me. The first thing I noticed was that I was hungry all the time. I started los-ing weight. It seemed like I had to urinate more frequently. I felt weak and tired all the time, too.

I chalked all of this up to food that was terrible and scarce, impossible sleeping conditions, no exercise, no fresh air, and an abundance of boredom. Those were certainly contributing fac-tors, especially the deficiencies in my diet. But my conditions were symptomatic of early onset diabetes. Only I didn't know it. Diabetes and its symptoms were unfamiliar to me, so I didn't make the connection.

Plus, prisoners don't have regular doctor visits. As a result, the health problems stemming from my diet went unaddressed. Meantime, other health problems arose. I started feeling sharp pains in my chest. I feared I was going to have a heart attack. On a couple of occasions I thought I might have suffered minor ones. But I kept telling myself that I was too young for a heart attack.

When my heart would act up, I'd lie on the floor and stay there. Sometimes I thought I was going to die from heart failure.

With so many health problems, I hit rock bottom. I didn't feel like doing anything. I'd stare at the ceiling for hours. I couldn't help thinking that I wouldn't be in this mess if I hadn't become a Christian. I had accepted Christ as my Savior. Since then I had lost my fiancé. My father had disowned me. My mother had killed herself. I was in prison on trumped-up charges. And after all that, my health was failing.

Meantime, where was God?

I was dwelling on this one night when a guard opened my cell and pushed in a prisoner. The guy had pale white skin, blond hair, and blue eyes. He was twenty-something. "He's staying the night," the guard said.

I'd seen this sort of thing before. Every once in a while a foreigner would be arrested and thrown in with the general prison population overnight. Then in the morning he'd be taken to court, and you'd never see him again. This guy was one of those cases. And it was pretty obvious that he was frightened.

"You will have no problem here," I told him. "You can relax."

He didn't say anything.

"What is your case?" I asked.

"I was arrested on immigration violations," he said. "I am a tourist."

"You should pray," I said. I'm not sure where that came from. I just said it.

He looked at me funny.

"Do you have a Bible?" I asked.

"Not on me."

"I have a King James Version."

"You are a Christian?"

"Yes."

"I am Simon. I'm from London."

245

"I'm Tito from Nigeria."

We ended up talking all night. He knew a lot about the persecution of Christians throughout the Middle East. He said he belonged to a nonprofit organization dedicated to helping Christians who are persecuted for their beliefs. The organization was called Christian Solidarity Worldwide (CSW), and it was based in England. I had never heard of the group. But one of CSW's main areas of emphasis was conducting public awareness campaigns to free Christians who had been jailed or imprisoned for their beliefs.

Before this Englishman was released, he told me how to contact CSW. I wrote the organization a letter and explained my situation. I reported that I had been arrested for converting to Christianity and sentenced to life in prison in Egypt. I sent the letter to the organization's headquarters in London. To my surprise, I received a response. It came from a woman who volunteered for the organization. She informed me that she planned to make my situation known to Christians around the world.

I was pretty skeptical. This was 1997, well before Facebook, Twitter, and YouTube. Very few people around the world even had e-mail at that time.

Just as I expected, nothing happened—at first. Then one day a guard informed me that I had mail. I sat up and rubbed my eyes. He handed me the envelope. It was postmarked from Greece. For a moment I just stared in disbelief. I didn't know anyone in Greece.

Slowly, I tore open the envelope and removed the letter.

Dear Tito,

Hello in Christ . . .

I always remember you and pray for you. Who knows? Maybe our Lord permitted your imprisonment so that you'll be able to know Him better; to love Him more. His wills are unexplored. But we are sure about one thing: That He is thinking of us.

A Christian minister had signed it. My eyes welled up. Some stranger in a faraway land had taken the time to write me. She spoke as if she knew me. Her letter gave me something to do. I wrote her back.

Within weeks, more letters came. They were from strangers, too. Christians from various parts of Europe were reaching out to me. I spent my days writing back to them. The more I wrote, the more letters I received. Pretty soon I couldn't keep up. A few letters turned into hundreds of letters. They just kept coming and coming. I discovered that there was a worldwide network of concerned Christians dedicated to helping individuals suffering religious persecution. Most of the letters addressed to me had come from England, Ireland, and the United States. Christians from around the world reached out to me.

Around the time I started getting all this mail from Christians, I got a cell assignment change. I was moved into José's cell. By this time he and I had become the best of friends. Being cell mates gave us a lot more opportunities to talk. I also discovered that he was a poet and a prolific writer. He kept a leather-bound journal and wrote all sorts of things in it.

He was pretty impressed by the volume of mail I was getting from other Christians. I was so encouraged that I decided to reestablish contact with the Mormon congregation in Cairo. With my health deteriorating, I knew I needed some medical attention from doctors outside the prison system. I figured the members from my old church might be the best equipped to help me.

I sent letter after letter to people I knew from the Mormon congregation. I mailed them all to the meetinghouse in Cairo. None of my letters were answered, though. Not one.

"I think I've been excommunicated," I told José.

"Excommunicated?"

"Nobody from the church will contact me."

"That doesn't mean you've been excommunicated."

"But it's not like them to cut off one of their own. I know these people."

"How do you know they've cut you off?"

"How do I know they haven't?"

"You need to trust God," José said.

A few days after this conversation, José and I were in our cell, writing letters. A guard opened the door. "Momen, you have a visitor."

I followed the guard to the visiting area. When I got there I didn't see anyone I recognized. "Who is the visitor?" I asked.

"That guy right there," the guard said, pointing to a man wearing traditional Muslim clothing.

"There must be some mix-up," I said. "I've never seen that man in my life."

"Well, he says he knows you."

I walked up to the man, folded my arms, and stared at him.

"We have a mutual friend," the stranger said.

Skeptical and mad at the world, I didn't say anything.

"Look," he said, "I came here to help you."

Prisons are full of con artists, liars, and backstabbers. When you are surrounded by this kind of people all the time, you get jaded. So when a guy showed up out of the blue and said he was a friend of a friend who wanted to help, I couldn't help being suspicious.

"How can you help me?" I said.

"Well, there must be something you need."

When I looked this guy in the eye, I couldn't help wanting to trust him.

"Thank you for coming to see me," I said.

We started talking. I ended up telling him about my recent

failed attempts to reestablish contact with the Mormon church in Cairo.

"That's something I might be able to help with," he said.

"Would you take a letter to the place where they meet?"

"I can do that."

I couldn't believe it. Here was a Muslim who was a complete stranger showing up at the prison and agreeing to help me establish contact with a Christian church in Cairo.

I put together a written message, indicating my condition and my whereabouts, asking why no one had answered my letters, and asking if I had been excommunicated. I handed it to my visitor. He said he'd do his best to deliver the message.

A few weeks later the man returned with a handwritten letter from the leader of the Mormon congregation in Cairo. The letter explained why my previous letters had gone unanswered—they were never received. The congregation had relocated. I had been sending mail to the old address, and my letters had not been forwarded.

I shared the news with José. "The best thing is that the letter made no mention of excommunication," I said.

"I told you not to worry."

"Church members had actually been trying to reach me. But prison officials apparently rebuffed their attempts. They had even tried to get me things to read. Everything was rejected."

My new Muslim friend stepped up again. He said he was willing to act as an intermediary between the Mormon congregation and me. That gesture enabled me to reestablish limited contact with my church.

I was so encouraged that I decided to write a letter directly to Gordon B. Hinckley, the head of the Mormon church in Salt Lake City, Utah. I did that just before Christmas in 1998. Members of The Church of Jesus Christ of Latter-day Saints considered Gordon B. Hinckley to be a living prophet. Mormons referred to him as President Hinckley. My writing to him was a bit like a Catholic writing directly to the pope.

I didn't actually expect to hear back. But I did. I received a letter from President Hinckley's personal secretary dated January 26, 1999. It was sent directly to the prison and said that President Hinckley had read my letter, appreciated my expressions of faith, and encouraged me to keep the faith.

The letter was a big boost. And it came just in time. Right afterward, I suffered a stroke. A cardiologist was dispatched to my cell, and he had me transferred to a hospital on February 15, 1999. Over the next few days I was diagnosed with congestive heart failure. My symptoms were shortness of breath, coughing, swelled ankles, rapid pulse, trouble sleeping, fatigue, and loss of appetite. The fatigue and the shortness of breath were probably the most acute. My body was just a mess. The cardiologist recommended open-heart surgery.

When an inmate in the Egyptian prison system needs a medical operation, he's on his own. Very few inmates have the resources to pay for procedures. But in my case, members of Christian Solidarity Worldwide offered to pay for the procedure. They even had a surgeon in England who was willing to travel to Egypt to perform the operation. But prison officials refused to approve the procedure.

One night I was lying awake, thinking that without the surgery I probably would die soon. My mind drifted to Aaban. The last time I saw her was when we brushed past each other in a Cairo hotel shortly after my mother's suicide. At that time, I was so furious with her that I couldn't stand to look at her. We had been so close. We had almost gotten married.

Lying in prison, I couldn't deny that I had wronged her. I was unfaithful to her. More than once. There are powers in us that we just have to suppress, but I hadn't. And she knew it.

Everybody knew how much she loved me. Nobody had ever loved me as Aaban did. Yet I had disappointed her. I had hurt her.

I couldn't get her face out of my mind. So I got up, found a pen and paper, and wrote a simple letter:

> Dearest Aaban, the love of my life,
>
> I have congestive heart failure, and I have to have open-heart surgery. I don't know if I will make it. I may never see you again. There are a couple of things I want to say. I forgive you for everything. I hope you will forgive me, too. And if you have the desire to write, please feel free. I am missing you.
>
> With all my best wishes and all my love,
> Muhammad

I still remembered her parents' address in Cairo. I mailed the letter there. I never got a response. I don't know if the letter even reached her.

The open-heart surgery never took place. Instead, I remained in the hospital until I recovered from the stroke. During that time I was allowed to receive regular visits from the leaders of the Mormon congregation in Cairo. They were permitted to give me a healing blessing. They were also allowed to bring me scriptures and church periodicals to read during recovery.

While I remained hospitalized, I wrote another letter to President Gordon B. Hinckley in Salt Lake City. I updated him on my medical condition and thanked him for his support. Not too long after I sent it I received a package at the hospital. It had come from Salt Lake City and contained a leather-bound edition of the Bible and the Book of Mormon. It had been sent by President Hinckley's office.

I also received a letter from a program specialist with the church's social services office in Salt Lake City. The letter informed me that church headquarters in Salt Lake City was in direct contact with local church leaders in Cairo about my condition.

"Remember, Brother Momen, the Lord knows you by name. He loves you without limitation. May the Lord bless you with the faith to follow Him and do His will."

The words of encouragement gave me the desire to persevere.

CHAPTER 31

MY FLORENCE NIGHTINGALE

By May of 1999, I had left the hospital and returned to my cell with José. From that point on I was permitted to see a heart specialist once a week. I was also put on medication for my heart. Individuals from the Mormon church would visit the prison every Saturday and drop off my medicines.

By the end of 1999, I was receiving regular, scheduled visits from church members. The visits and letters gave me a sense of connection to the outside world.

One of my visitors was an American woman named Mary. Her husband had taken a temporary job in Cairo, and they attended Mormon church meetings there. In the summer of 1999, they spotted on the bulletin board of the meeting place my picture and a notice about my medical condition. Other than that, they knew nothing about me.

A leader of the congregation asked Mary if she'd be willing to take medication to me on Saturdays, the one day for inmate visits. The men in the Mormon congregation had trouble getting away from work on Saturdays to visit me in prison. Between travel time and lengthy processing procedures to get in and out of the prison facility, it wasn't unusual to use up an entire day to accomplish a fifteen-minute visit.

The thought of going to see an inmate in Kanater frightened Mary. She had never been inside an American prison, let alone an Egyptian one. But Mary wasn't going to reject an invitation to help someone in need.

On October 23, 1999, Mary visited me for the first time. She came with three other women from the Maadi Christian Church in Cairo. One of them, called Elizabeth, had been visiting me and other Christian inmates for years. She knew the procedures and guided Mary through the process.

I was pretty sick and weak the day they came. I was waiting in "the cage," the designated space for visitors to meet inmates. The cage was a heavily guarded room with a concrete floor, concrete benches, concrete walls, and a false ceiling of chicken wire over the top.

Elizabeth led Mary in and introduced us. Mary looked haggard and nervous. The environment was a little overwhelming for her. The cage was crowded with Arab and African inmates, along with their visitors. The journey to reach the prison had been unsettling, too. Mary had traveled over an hour through some pretty undesirable areas, including a district of factories and large outdoor kilns with huge smoke stacks that belched out smog. Once at the prison she was required to wait another ninety minutes in a filthy waiting area with sand-covered floors, grimy windows, and stifling heat. Then her bags were searched, and she was frisked.

Elizabeth and the other two women from the Maadi Christian Church were used to all this. Not Mary. She flashed a nervous smile and said that she had brought me some gifts: new pairs of socks, a sweatshirt, some produce, candy, milk, and a container of Nestlé Quik chocolate powder. She had been told that I loved chocolate milk. She also gave me a week's worth of medication for my heart.

Mary had no idea why I was in prison. I gave her an abbreviated account. We had only about fifteen minutes before the guards sent Mary out, and I had to return to my cell.

Mary nursed me through some dark days. Her courage and self-less sacrifice reminded me of Florence Nightingale, the English-born Anglican who believed she had been called by God to be a nurse. Nightingale attended to injured soldiers in the Crimean War and later took her travels to Egypt. She was in Cairo in 1850 when she wrote in her diary: "God called me in the morning & asked me 'Would I do good for Him, for Him alone without reputation.'"

That's how Mary felt about her service to me. Her prison visits continued until she returned to the United States in 2000, and then we stayed in touch by writing each other on a regular basis.

One day I was reading my Book of Mormon and José was reading his Bible. We were in our cell. He turned to me. "So what is different about that book from the Bible?"

"They are pretty similar," I said.

"But what's different?"

I thought for a moment. José was an intellectual and an avid reader. He'd read anything he could get his hands on.

"Would you like to read the Book of Mormon?" I asked. "That way you could see for yourself."

"I would like that."

I wasn't trying to convert him. But he knew I had been a Muslim and that I had converted to Mormonism. He was just in-stinctively curious about other Christian sects. I sent a letter to church headquarters in Salt Lake City and requested a Spanish edi-tion of the Book of Mormon. It arrived about six weeks later. José read it cover to cover in less than a week. Once he did that, our friendship deepened even more. I felt like José understood me better than anyone else in the prison.

In 2000, a number of Turkish inmates in my prison were granted clemency by the Egyptian government and were released. We who were non-Egyptian inmates were encouraged by this. I began to hope that I might get an early release from prison, too. By the end of 2000, I wrote a letter to President Mubarak asking for clemency.

Mubarak never responded. During the first half of 2001, I wrote him a half dozen more letters, each one petitioning for a release due to my medical condition. Every letter went unanswered, but I still hoped.

The period between summer 1999 and fall 2001 was probably the smoothest since I had entered the prison system. I had weekly checkups with a doctor, weekly visits from members of the Mormon church, and lots of incoming and outgoing mail. It doesn't get much better than that behind bars.

Then everything changed.

Most people I know remember where they were on September 11, 2001. I'll never forget where I was when I first discovered that America was under attack. I saw a gathering of inmates around the television. Everyone was silent. I approached just in time to see a plane crashing into the World Trade Center. I didn't understand what I was seeing. None of us did at first.

But when the first tower came down, the atmosphere in my cell block turned hysterical. The inmates started shouting and cheering. They danced, raised their fists in the air, and rattled the bars of the prison cells. They chanted anti-American slogans. By the time the second tower came down, the celebration inside the prison had reached fever pitch. The inmates were more out of control than fans at a World Cup soccer match. The pressure to go along with the crowd was immense. I was too sick to my stomach to cheer and too afraid not to. Anybody who didn't go along was likely to be seen as an American sympathizer.

Amidst the chaos I slipped back to my cell and pretended I was too ill to come out. In some respects, it wasn't an act. I was horrified when I saw innocent people jumping to their death from those buildings. The inmates, however, were furious that they weren't free to help carry out the attacks. They chanted anti-American slogans. They vowed to do violence. This went on all day and into the night. It was not a good day to be a Christian in the prison. All I could do that night was pray. But I didn't dare kneel. I lay on my cot, closed my eyes, and cried.

My circumstances changed immediately. Many of the Mormons in Cairo were Americans. Almost all of them left Egypt and returned to the United States. The few that remained were no longer allowed into the prison. I tried writing letters to those who had gone home. But U.S. officials were not accepting mail from Egypt, at least not letters from my prison.

For months I couldn't receive letters from the States, either. Even the Christian women who regularly visited the prison were no longer allowed in. I felt cut off and lost without the correspondence and visits from my Christian friends.

Finally, after six months, one of my letters reached Mary in Virginia. And her letters started reaching me again. At that point I became a prolific letter writer.

———

July 5, 2002

Dear Mary,

The weather is arid hot these couple days, especially when we are locked in for the night. The cells are unbearable. We lost two lives last week, one in my room at 1:30 a.m. Lack of ventilation. He spent twenty-four and a half years in here. He was from Lebanon.

————

October 6, 2002

Dear Mary,

I am grateful to the Lord for providing medications and for giving me the strength to accept my illness and learn how to live with it.

Now I can say our Heavenly Father has a purpose for me to be here. And as my life goes on and my doing time in here is mingled with new challenges, I've learned to rely on our Savior to find solace. . . .

Elizabeth finds it difficult to visit her inmates. Actually, since Sept. 11, '01, things are never the same in here.

————

December 9, 2002

Dear Mary,

The Christian visits were completely stopped last week. It was terrible. They need special permission from the Prison Department. Please pray that the Lord will touch the hearts of the authorities that they may allow the visits.

I wish you every blessing on this joyous Christmas Day. Even though we will be thousands of miles apart, warm thoughts will keep you near.

Best wishes and all my love and prayers. May you be blessed in the New Born King.

MY FLORENCE NIGHTINGALE

February 2, 2003

Dear Mary,

Since September 11, things are getting worse in here. And now with the possible war on Iraq, the hardship is increasing on us.

July 1, 2003

Dear Mary,

It was great to have . . . the restriction lifted to facilitate the visits. Since then I had two visits from the Cairo congregation and I'm expecting the third this month. Praise the Lord!

About two years after 9/11, a new chief of security was appointed at Kanater. It turned out to be the Coptic Christian guard I had met when I arrived at Tora and who escorted me to the terrorist-turned-imam. We had become friends during my first year of incarceration, but then he was reassigned to another prison, and I had not seen him since. The news that the only Christian guard I had ever encountered in the prison system was in charge of every other guard came as a pleasant surprise. I thanked God.

José was pretty ecstatic, too. So were the four other Christian prisoners in our cell block. The six of us were a pretty distinct minority amongst three hundred Muslim inmates. The six of us weren't Arabs, either, whereas most of the inmates were. To maintain solidarity, the six of us decided to meet informally every Friday to talk about religion. Our cell block had a television that was typically tuned to Al Jazeera. So sometimes we also discussed politics in our Friday meetings.

All six of us looked for ways to advance ourselves despite being in prison. One day I said to the group that a prison is just a building. We could act like most prisoners and just waste our time in it, or we could look at the prison as something else. It could be a church or a school or even an art studio. My point was that we could either let the building destroy us or we could choose to be productive.

That was the beginning of a revolutionary change in the way we spent our time in prison. Some guys started studying pretty heavily. I started teaching a weekly Bible class. Then we came up with an idea to do arts and crafts. Most of us were artistically inclined and had some talent. We went to the prison authorities and said that we wanted to start a workshop. We made the case that it would improve prison morale and encourage inmates to be more productive. It would also cut down on violence and insubordination.

Eventually, the prison officials went along with the idea. They had just one condition. We had to build the workshop ourselves. The prison supplied the materials, and we constructed a small workspace akin to a shed. It was pretty rudimentary, but it was functional. We outfitted it with a few easels and such art supplies as paint, brushes, pencils, and sketch pads. We accumulated these things over time, not all at once. Eventually, I got to a point where I was sketching or painting almost daily.

For the most part I did religious paintings. I portrayed Christian scenes and Muslim scenes. José painted too. We set our easels beside each other, and the two of us would talk while we painted. A couple of the prison ministers saw my work and asked me to make postcard-sized prints. I did, and the ministers took my prints to a church bazaar held every weekend at a hotel in downtown Cairo. The prints were sold there. So I started making a little money, which enabled me to purchase more art supplies and various food items.

Eventually, members of the Mormon congregation in Cairo

started taking my prints and shipping them to the United States, where they were sold to other Mormons. The proceeds were deposited in a bank account that was established in my behalf by a Mormon businessman in Texas. All the money was dedicated to help me transition back into society after I was released from prison and to help me get settled in a community outside of Egypt.

It was still far from certain that I'd actually make it out of prison. Christian groups targeted the Nigerian embassy, campaigning for my release, and the diplomat assigned to my petition was working on my behalf. But many hurdles remained.

CHAPTER 32

A BAD YEAR

Early in 2004, I woke up one morning and couldn't feel my toes on my left foot. Even when I walked there was no feeling. The left side of my face felt funny, too. Then I tried lifting my left hand to touch my face. It was as if my hand were dead. No mobility. But my right hand worked just fine.

Luckily for me, I had a visit scheduled with the cardiologist that day. When he observed my condition, he explained that I had likely suffered another stroke. This one seemed more serious than the one I had had a few years earlier. The inability to feel or use parts of the left side of my body scared me.

Before the end of the day, a nurse had taken blood and urine samples from me. They were sent to an outside lab for testing. The nurse didn't work for the prison, and he seemed pretty friendly. He told me that one of the things they were looking for was evidence of diabetes.

While I waited for the results to come back, I searched for any information I could find on diabetes. I came across an article in an old magazine. It listed the symptoms of a diabetic. I had most of them, including partial loss of vision. I had been having trouble with my eyes for some time. Things would appear blurry. Sometimes my eyes wouldn't focus. Not all the time, though. Still, I noticed that these bouts of blurriness were getting more frequent and lasting longer.

A prison doctor eventually confirmed that I had diabetes, and he prescribed daily injections of insulin. Being a diabetic anywhere is no fun, but being a diabetic in prison is hell. One of the problems is that prisoners have to pay for their own medications. That meant I had to buy my own insulin. There was a private contractor who visited the prison regularly with insulin to sell to inmates. So I had access to insulin. The challenge was coming up with the cash.

All inmates face this challenge. The thing that saved me was my artwork. Besides having my prints sold in the United States by my Mormon friends, by 2004 my sketches and paintings were also being sold pretty regularly by Christian ministries in the United Kingdom. This was set up through the Anglican church. The pastor of the Anglican church in Cairo would take my artwork and send it to England, where it was distributed and sold. The proceeds from these sales were then sent back to the Anglican pastor in Cairo, who put money in an account at the prison. I used that money to buy my insulin.

The job of administering my daily insulin injections fell to José. Eventually, I resumed my painting. One day José and I were painting side by side in the art room when a guard appeared. "José, you have a visitor."

José put down his paintbrush and wiped his hands. "I'll be back soon," he said to me.

An hour later he was back. Without saying a word, he sat down and resumed painting.

"Who came to visit you?" I asked.

"Someone from the Spanish consulate."

I glanced over at him. Tears were streaming down his face.

"What's going on?" I asked.

He didn't say a word. He just kept painting.

"José?"

"I will tell you when we get back to our cell."

"Tell me now. You are worrying me."

He put down his brush. "The consulate official said my clemency has been granted."

"And you are crying? I don't understand."

The inmate on the other side of me overheard our conversation. He was from Colombia. "José is going!" he shouted. "José is going."

There were half a dozen inmates in the art room that day. They started clapping. I was thrilled for José, too.

José didn't smile.

"This is what you wanted," I said to José.

He got up and walked out.

I followed him to our cell.

"What is the problem?" I asked.

"This isn't the first time I've been told I was being released. Each time the release has fallen through."

"You're afraid that will happen again?"

"Yes."

"Remember what you told me?"

"What?"

"You have to have faith."

Two nights later, two guards showed up at our cell. It was during the dinner hour. Guys were eating and talking. Over the din of conversation, one of the guards shouted: "José, pack your things. You are leaving in the morning."

Everyone in our cell stopped. Then they rose to their feet and started chanting. "José is going. José is going. José is going."

Men started banging on the cell bars with cooking pots and utensils.

The enthusiasm spread to the neighboring cells. Within moments, the entire cell block was chanting. "José is going. José is going. José is going."

Tears streamed down José's face. Even the guards started chanting. I threw my arms around José. I could feel his tears on my neck.

He spent the rest of the night giving away his books, his cigarettes, and his food supplies. We hardly slept that night. No one in our cell did. The next morning all the prisoners lined the corridor when the guards came to get José. When José emerged from his cell, the men started shouting: "José! José! José! José! José!"

The noise was deafening. All these hardened criminals had tears in their eyes. The most beloved man in our prison had finally gotten his freedom. He took the time to hug and shake hands with everyone as he made his way down the line. I was at the end of the line. We threw our arms around each other for the last time.

"Be strong, Tito," he said, weeping. "I don't know where I'm going. But I promise to call."

"At least you are free. Anywhere is better than an Egyptian jail."

"You will be in my prayers, Tito."

I watched him pass through the iron doors and disappear. I cried with joy and sadness.

CHAPTER 33

A GOOD YEAR

I said good-bye to José near the end of 2004. Without my best friend, I was lost. My whole outlook changed. I rarely left my cell. I had sunk into an abyss. For the first time in my life, I entertained thoughts of suicide. I was just so utterly lonely and defeated.

But I had a cell mate from Zaire, and one day I overheard him talking about a diplomat from Niger who was helping him apply for clemency. At one point he said the diplomat's name: Muhammad Donle. I knew that name. I had attended primary school with Muhammad's brother in Nigeria, and I knew that my classmate's younger brother had become a diplomat with the Niger embassy.

I immediately decided to get in touch with Donle. The reason he was so sought after was that most sub-Saharan African diplomats didn't speak Arabic. That put African inmates at a big disadvantage, since everything in Egypt is done in Arabic. But Donle was fluent in Arabic.

I knew he'd help me if I could just get his attention. It took a few tries, but with the other inmates' help I was eventually able to reach Donle on the telephone. He shouted for joy when he heard my voice. He said he had heard all kinds of stories about me. He promised his full support to help me obtain an early release.

Within a week Donle showed up at the prison. The first thing he did was apply for a permit that would enable members of the Mormon church to make more frequent visits of longer duration. I'd had no idea this option existed.

Next he filed a petition with President Mubarak seeking clemency for me. I explained that I had already petitioned the Egyptian president close to a dozen times and never received as much as an acknowledgment that my letters had been received. But Donle assured me that my medical condition qualified me for an early release under medical hardship. As he put it, my strokes and diabetes were a good thing. He said I should thank God for them.

I took his advice. I thanked God. Meantime, Donle did more than petition the Egyptian government for clemency. He went to the Nigerian embassy and started putting backdoor pressure on the Egyptian consulate. At the same time, the Christian Solidarity Worldwide stepped up its public campaign to have me and other Christian inmates released. Other human rights organizations got involved. And thanks to Donle's efforts, representatives from the Mormon congregation in Cairo were able to spend more time with me in prison, enabling us to start mapping out a transition plan to help me settle in Ghana once my release was secured.

Before I knew it, I was behaving as if I were definitely going to be released. My whole outlook underwent a change. So did my physical appearance. My paralysis lifted. I actually regained the use of my limbs on my left side. From a medical perspective I couldn't really explain this, and neither could the doctors. But men from the Mormon church administered to me. At the same time, Christians from all over the world were praying for me. I believe the collective blessings and prayers of these good people had a lot to do with my healing.

My spirits were lifted. I had hope again. Hope has a way of being self-perpetuating. Hope breeds faith. And faith produces miracles.

CHAPTER 34

REDEMPTION

In March of 2006, I was in the art room painting when one of my fellow inmates approached me. "The major wants to see you," the inmate said. "He has good news for you. He said to get his sweets ready."

I looked toward the door. The major was standing there in a military uniform. He had an eagle patch on the sleeve. He had a big mustache, dark hair, and bright white teeth. I put down my paintbrush and walked toward him.

"My uncle," he said, "where are my sweets?"

"They are ready," I said. "Just tell me the news."

"Your paper is ready," he said. "I just brought in your red card."

I was dumbstruck. I couldn't speak.

"You should be happy," the major said.

I started crying. "Are you sure?"

"I brought it myself. You know me. I don't lie."

He gave me a kiss on both cheeks. "Congratulations."

"I will give you twenty Egyptian pounds!" I said.

Instantly, the other men in the art room started emptying their pockets and giving whatever they had—money, cigarettes, candy—to the major.

On April 7, 2006, a member of the Mormon congregation in Cairo showed up at the prison and provided me with civilian clothes: a white business shirt with red stripes, a jacket, khaki pants, a necktie, shoes, and socks. The next morning I got up, showered, and dressed. I hadn't worn a tie in over fifteen years. When I looked in the mirror, I didn't recognize myself. I looked respectable.

Am I really this person? I thought.

I didn't have much time to contemplate the question. Three other prisoners were being released with me that day—one Egyptian, one Nigerian, and one Syrian. When the guards appeared in our wing, I heard one of them shout: "Tito, come out."

Instantly, the men in our wing started chanting: "Tito! Tito! Tito! Tito!"

I emerged from my cell dressed in business casual attire. All the prisoners were whistling and clapping and shouting.

"Get out of here," one inmate shouted. "You are not needed here anymore, Momen."

People were hugging and kissing me. I looked at their faces and wept. I knew so many of them would die there. One inmate I couldn't stand approached. He hugged me. I hugged him. And we wept.

I had lived with these men for fifteen years. Ate with them. Slept with them. Suffered with them. I didn't realize how much I loved them.

The guards led me to the doors that led outside. The sun was just coming up over the horizon. It was so bright I had to shield my eyes.

"Good luck," one of the guards said.

I looked over my shoulder at the crowd of prisoners, so many of them, in blue uniforms, waving from inside the barbed wire fence.

My last day as an inmate was April 8, 2006. The next day, a Sunday, I appeared before a judge.

He glanced at some papers and then up at me.

"What is your name?"

"Tito Momen."

Then he looked at the papers again before saying that I owed a fine. "Do you plan on paying it?"

I reminded the judge that I had been in prison for fifteen years and therefore couldn't possibly come up with the money to pay the fine. I also told him that I had no family in Egypt. And I was sick with a heart condition and diabetes.

I kept on talking until he finally cut me off. There was a long silence while he flipped back through the documents in his hands. Then he looked up and asked me about my conversion to Christianity. He wanted to know if I'd make the same decision again.

I hadn't expected to be asked that. But the question convinced me that what I had thought all along was true: I had been punished for my religious beliefs. I knew it. There was something in the judge's papers that proved it. How else would he have known to ask me about it?

I told him that I would make the same decision again.

"After all the suffering you have experienced?" the judge pressed.

"Yes."

The judge had two advisers with him, one to his left and one to his right. I didn't know if they were lawyers or clerks, but the judge consulted with them in private. Then he faced me again. He told me that if he released me, I would have to leave Egypt at once. And I was never to return. He said, "Go, and never look back."

With the help of the Nigerian embassy and individual members

271

of the Mormon church, I landed in Ghana shortly after my release from prison. Unlike in Egypt, Mormonism was flourishing in Ghana. Church members there were on hand to greet me at the airport. They helped me find housing. They bought me groceries, helped me look for employment, and provided me with money during the interim. They even gave me a used computer and set me up with an e-mail account. I had never even heard of e-mail.

In many respects, leaving prison is like stepping out of a time warp. For fifteen years the world had been moving on while I stayed still. Technology had advanced. People had aged. Relationships had changed. The world was a different place. But I was settling in, and the first few months of freedom flew by.

Then on a hot September day in 2006, I was in the back of a taxi that was passing through a busy intersection in Ghana's capital city, Accra. The traffic forced us to stop. That's when I heard a man shouting. It took me a moment to realize that the man was shouting at the driver of my cab, demanding that he pull off to the shoulder.

The man on the street looked vaguely familiar. Then he looked at me through the rear window and shouted my name: "Muhammad!"

I hadn't been called that name in nearly twenty years. But I instantly recognized the voice. It was my cousin from Nigeria—the same cousin who had accompanied me to school in Damascus and to the university in Cairo. The same one who had started all of my troubles in Egypt and back home by telling everyone that I had converted to Christianity. If there was one man most responsible for my years in prison, it was this man.

A familiar fear swept over me as soon as our eyes met. I wanted to speed away. But we were in bumper-to-bumper traffic. I was stuck.

My cousin approached the cab. My heart started racing. *Why is he here?* I wondered. I rolled down my window.

"Your father is dying," he said.

At first I didn't feel anything. In some ways, my father had been dead to me for a long time. He and my stepbrothers had wanted me dead. Largely because of them I had spent a good part of my life in prison.

Still, the suggestion that he might be about to leave this world gave me pause.

"Your father is dying," my cousin repeated. "And he wants to see you."

That made me suspicious. There was no way my father wanted to see me. My family had held a public funeral for me in 1989, two years before I went to prison. In their eyes, I had died when I became a Christian. My father had disowned me right around the time my mother killed herself. Why would he want to see me now?

My cousin insisted he was telling the truth.

I didn't trust him.

Yet if he was telling the truth, I had to return to Nigeria. I had to see my father one last time before he died.

"He wants to see you," my cousin repeated.

I stepped out of the cab. What if this whole thing was a ruse to get me to go back there? I could be a dead man if I went home. I looked my cousin in the eyes. I considered him to be the lowest form of human life on earth. I despised what he had done to me. I didn't trust him. I think he sensed all of those things from my expression.

But standing there in that intersection, I decided to trust a man I didn't trust. Something told me he was telling me the truth. I vowed to return home before it was too late.

It had been approximately seventeen years since I had visited the village where I was raised in Nigeria. When I arrived, I could tell that things had changed. The countryside and the buildings were the same. And there was still a lot of poverty. But the mood was different. It was darker, more ominous. All the men were dressed like the Taliban. All the women were wearing veils. Most of the boys I had grown up with were now judges and clerics. They had all embraced Osama Bin Laden.

The Taliban had gained a foothold in my homeland. Fortunately, I had made a point of outfitting myself in Islamic attire before I left Ghana. Otherwise, I would have had a real problem on my hands. Nonetheless, I was still very uneasy. Most people knew I was a Christian. I didn't feel safe.

I went directly to the hospital. I had no idea what to expect. When I entered my father's room, I found him sleeping on his hospital bed. His mouth was open, his breathing labored. His face was hollow and his eyes sunken. His paper-thin skin barely covered his bones. He was bald, emaciated, and frail.

This is the man I feared my whole life? I thought.

I stood there gazing at him for a few minutes.

Then his eyes opened, and he recognized me. A peaceful smile came over his face. I'd never seen that smile before.

"My son," he whispered.

I approached slowly. We stared at each other in silence. Then he reached for my hand. His touch felt frail. I leaned over the bed to get closer to him.

"Now that I see you," he whispered, "Allah has answered my prayer. I asked Allah that if what you believe in is true, I should see your face before I died. Allah has shown me your face. So I believe in whatever you believe in."

Was I hearing things? Was my father senile?

"Is it too late for me?" he asked. He sounded so desperate, so pathetic.

By that point I was an emotional mess. My father had made me cry many times in my lifetime. But this was the first time the tears were born of sympathy. I could see the fear in his eyes.

"It's never too late," I said. "Father in Heaven is a God of mercy."

He looked in my eyes. I took his hand.

"Christ died for everyone. Everyone can be redeemed, Father."

"The Lord you're worshipping will take care of me?" he pleaded.

Too choked up to speak, I just nodded.

We talked for two hours that day. It was the best conversation I ever had with my father. It was the last time I saw him alive. He died later that afternoon.

I never thought I'd cry when my father died, but I wept like a baby. I miss him terribly. What I really miss is what we never had. I would have spent another fifteen years in prison in exchange for the opportunity to be close to my father as a boy. I so badly wanted to please him. I wanted to hear his praise. I wanted to kick a soccer ball with him. I wanted to paint him a picture and have him tell me he liked it. I wanted to tell him I met a girl and fell in love. I wanted to ask him for advice. I wanted to talk to him about something other than religion. I wanted him to say something to make me laugh. I wanted him to put his hand on my shoulder and tell me about a time when he made a mistake as a boy. I wanted to see him kiss my mother. I wanted to be his boy. Most of all, I wanted him to want me.

The next time I see him will be on the other side. I do believe he'll be there. At that point he won't be a Muslim and I won't be a Christian. We will simply be children of God. I fully expect that he will open his arms and I will accept his embrace. It will be sweeter than any embrace I have felt in this life.

My mother will be there, too. I expect her to be at my father's side. She will be proud of me. She will know what I believe. And she will be forever grateful.

I stayed in Nigeria until my father received a proper Islamic burial. With all the rituals, that took forty days. Being in the place where I grew up was an exercise in depression. But it was also one of the best experiences of my life. Being there gave me the perspective to see just how far I had come and how fortunate I'd been.

There was a time when I felt guilty for womanizing and

becoming an alcoholic when I lived in Egypt. I did things I'm not proud of. But my trip home helped me get over that guilt once and for all. I recognized that those things were a necessary diversion from the path I was on. Without that diversion, I would never have embraced Christianity. I had to get to a point where I was searching for something else.

It would not be a stretch to say that I was snatched from the clutches of the Taliban. That became clear to me during my visit home. One night I was invited to the home of one of my childhood acquaintances. When I entered the house, they were raucously carrying on while watching a report on Al Jazeera television about the United States military presence in Iraq. They were praising Bin Laden for his attacks on the U.S. And they were eager for an opportunity to do their part.

The realization that all of my childhood peers were devoted to Al-Qaeda was a sobering one. That night I knelt down and thanked God that I had been thrown out of the institute in Syria after I hit my instructor. I thanked God that my professor at Al-Azhar had seized my notes and turned against me. Otherwise, I would have been like the rest of the men in my village. They paid homage to Osama Bin Laden. They believed that killing Americans was a fast track to heaven. None of them had any hesitation about stoning a disobedient woman to death. I had come chillingly close to being one of them.

When I boarded the plane to fly back to Ghana, I bade farewell to my homeland. I wouldn't be who I am if I had not come from that place. It's in me. But I'm glad I got out.

EPILOGUE

From New York, I took another flight to Salt Lake City. The Delta terminal in Salt Lake International Airport was packed when I walked off the air bridge. Mormons from across the world were gathering for the church's worldwide conference. As I made my way toward the baggage claim, I couldn't help thinking of the Muslim tradition of Hajj, pilgrimage to Mecca. Every Muslim man is expected to make that journey at least once in his lifetime.

For Mormons, going to Salt Lake City to participate in a worldwide conference is a bit like going to Mecca for Muslims. I had been longing to make this journey for a long time, and I was so excited I hadn't been able to eat or sleep while I traveled.

When I arrived at Temple Square, I found that the grandeur of the architecture and the overwhelming theme of Christ were unlike anything I'd seen in Africa. But I was most struck by the diversity of the church members in the streets. Most of the people who live in Utah are white. Yet at Temple Square I was surrounded by Hispanics, Africans, Asians, Europeans, and Pacific Islanders. People were speaking Japanese, Mandarin, Korean, Spanish, French, German, Portuguese, Italian, Greek, and even Arabic. I am a black African who used to be a Muslim, and I fit right in.

The Church of Jesus Christ of Latter-day Saints began with a fourteen-year-old boy in upstate New York who said he had a vision. That vision reached all the way to me, a boy who grew up in a small, remote village in Nigeria.

As I stood outside the Salt Lake Temple pondering all this, snow started to fall lightly. I had never seen snow.

I should have been cold. But I wasn't. I had goose bumps. But the temperature didn't trigger them.